Over the Sunset Mountain

A LIFE OF JOY AND FAITH

VIOLA SCHMIDT

 FriesenPress

Suite 300 - 990 Fort St
Victoria, BC, V8V 3K2
Canada

www.friesenpress.com

ISBN
978-1-5255-1142-4 (Hardcover)
978-1-5255-1143-1 (Paperback)
978-1-5255-1144-8 (eBook)

1. BIOGRAPHY & AUTOBIOGRAPHY

Distributed to the trade by The Ingram Book Company

This book is dedicated to my sister Alvina's two sons, David and Conrad. She would be very proud of you both.

Alvina loved music and I've named the book after one of her favourite Christian songs. Listen to its words and you will know the joy and faith she carried with her through her life.

TABLE OF CONTENTS

I. ALVINA — BABY

Alvina Rosie Bergman was born on July 2, 1937. Our mother, Justina (Derksen) Bergman was in the St. Paul's Hospital, Saskatoon, Saskatchewan in Canada. Mother was forty-three years old. At the time of Alvina's birth, her father, Peter Bergman, was in Winnipeg, Manitoba at the Canadian Mennonite Brethren Church conference. He was a delegate from the Borden MB church. During one of the sessions at the conference a telegram was received and read out to inform Father that he had a daughter. I'm sure he was hoping to have a son because Alvina had three older sisters, Esther, Helen, and me; Viola. Living on a farm, boys were a necessity. But it was not to be for the Bergmans.

The weather in July of 1937 was very hot — 104° — the hottest on record. No one had fans. There was no electrical power on the farms. To cool off you'd have to go into the cellar or the icehouse. Behind our house, under the trees, Father had dug a big hole, filled it with large blocks of ice during the winter, and put a shingled hip-roof over it. This was where we stored our butter, cream, and milk during the summer.

The crops on the Bergman quarter-sections of land were dried up. Father tried to convert the binder from a sheaves-pickup to picking up whatever short stems of crop could be retrieved. It was a depressing time.

In the meantime, it was fortunate that Alvina was born in the hospital. There were complications and she had to stay there a while. When she did come home, there were feeding problems. Father mentioned this when he went shopping for groceries at the Smith and McQuarrie store in the town of Borden. This was our nearest store — twelve miles from the farm. Father spoke to Norman Smith and he knew how to solve the problem. He suggested trying Mellin's Food. (Pablum had not been invented yet.) Father brought it home and Alvina loved it. From being under-weight, she blossomed into a cute, chubby baby. When she woke at night for her feeding, she wanted her bottle right "now." It took a while to warm the milk. The kerosene lamp had to be lit. Father had made a metal frame to fit over the glass lamp chimney and keep the milk (in a metal cup) in place while warming. By this time everyone in the house was awake. Alvina was an active and happy child. She loved to lie on the dining room table and kick her legs. I was assigned to the task of watching her. Playpens and mobiles were not to be found yet. I also remember rocking the wooden cradle to help Alvina fall asleep for naptime.

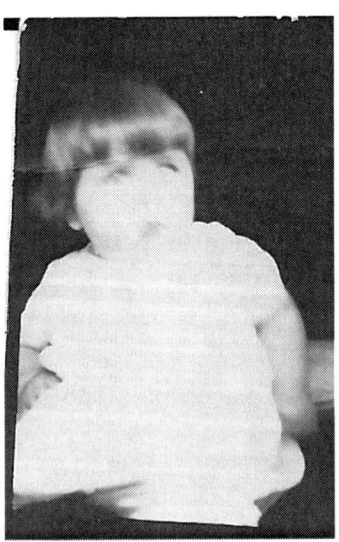

Alvina 6 months

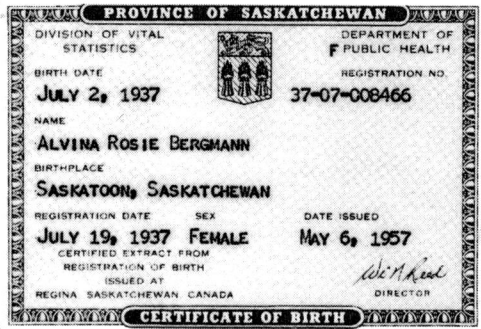

Certificate of Birth Card

Alvina's Birth Certificate

Alvina 2 years

Alvina was healthy and cute. Before long she could wander all over the farmyard, but her sisters were always near by. Chickens and a rooster or two also roamed the yard for food, often enjoying the potato and vegetable peelings that were provided for them.

Viola, Helen, and Alvina in the snow

Alvina is enjoying the snow along with Helen and me. The snowman is dressed up and looking stylish. Our dog, Buster, was enjoying our company.

Bergman Family — 1940

The family decided to take a formal picture in Saskatoon at Thams Studio. Dad and Mother weren't too happy with this picture, so didn't order more prints.

Bergman Family — 1941

Alvina was four or five years of age. Now this summer photo was more suitable to everyone's liking.

Take note, my sister Esther was a gifted seamstress. She had taken lessons and even knew how to make the patterns. (They were not available in stores in those days.) She sewed all of our dresses, fancy collars and all. She also cut our hair. She herself knew how to set waves and wore a fashionable bun, which was in style in those days. Before her wedding she got a haircut and a permanent wave.

During that summer of 1941, Helen and I were sick with the whooping cough. What a time that was! Father and Mother had planned a trip to B.C. to visit Mother's sister Margaret, who was married to John Stobbe. Grandmother Derksen planned to come with us. Finally, Helen and I were well enough to go. We drove the Canadian route and it was rather dangerous winding our way through the Rockies. Mother was particularly anxious and tense, which didn't help Father, who was focusing on keeping us safe. Out of the blue, Alvina started singing, "Gott verlasst die seinen nicht" (God does not forsake His own). We, as a family, had learned this song to present it at the Christian Endeavour program at church. Father had played the auto-harp and the rest of us sang our hearts out. Alvina remembered the melody along with the lyrics. We know it came from the Lord and was a huge encouragement to Mother, Father, and the rest of us. God kept us safe.

Later, on the way home, we took the United States route that provided safer, wider highways. We stayed in cabins during the night. We had to bring our own bedding, which we stored in a specially made rainproof bag and attached to the top of the car.

Oh yes, the reason Alvina sang her song in German—all our church services were conducted in the High German language. At home we spoke Low German. At school it was English. What a rich heritage we have in knowing several languages!

II. HALCYONIA SCHOOL

The location of our farm was in the district of the Halcyonia School — two miles directly south. Walking to school in the summer, we could cross the fields along the fence line. We'd cross our quarter section of land, then Buswell's quarter. Next it was Saunders field and lastly Pearce's.

Most of our neighbours south of us had come from England; city folk who were also searching for land. They arrived in 1904. If it had not been for the Doukhobors, who had settled in next door and taught them how to build clay ovens, bake bread, and plant gardens, they would have starved. The nearest grocery stores were in Saskatoon, fifty miles away. The only means to get there was with a team of horses or oxen.

By the time we Bergman girls went to the Halcyonia School, everyone was settled on farms and knew how to plant their crops and gardens and have a comfortable life.

Halcyonia School

Margaret Muirhead, Helen, and I on the way to school

Father built a two-wheeled cart and Fan, the horse, would take us on the roads, which were three and a half miles one-way.

Helen and I and Margaret Muirhead, our neighbour, are on the way to the Halcyonia School. Alvina was too young at this point to be going to school. During the winter we took a small covered sleigh, which Father also built for us girls.

Halcyonia School Students — 1943

This is the Halcyonia School student body of twenty children in the year of 1943 or 1944. Alvina is seven or eight years old. She is in the front row, on the right. Helen is in the third row from the bottom, second from the left.

III. THE BORDEN MENNONITE BRETHREN CHURCH

Borden Mennonite Brethren Church
(Photo copied from the book: Borden Mennonite Brethren Church *Precious Memories*– page 48 — Printed and bound in Canada by Friesen Printers, a Division of D.W. Friesen & Sons Ltd., Altona, Manitoba — 1980)

This is the Borden Mennonite Brethren Church. The Bergman family attended here. Men and women had separate entrance doors. Women sat on one side of the church and men on the other.

The church was three and three-quarter miles north of our farm. In the summertime we could use the car, but it was too cold during the winter and the roads were covered with snow. Father built a larger closed-in sleigh, which included a small stove to keep us warm.

Services were held every Sunday morning and often in the evening too. During the week, there would be an evening for young people's get-togethers and another evening of choir practice.

Alvina's Sunday School Class
(Photo copied from the book: Borden Mennonite Brethren
Church *Precious Memories* — page 40.)

The above picture shows Alvina with her Sunday school class. She is in the front row, second from the left. She's wearing a big smile.

Grandpa and Grandma Derksen's house

Here is our Grandparents Derksen's (Mother's parents) house on the farm. It was about two miles from our farm. This was a popular place.

Most every Sunday afternoon we would go and visit our grandparents' farm — meeting up with our uncles, aunts, and cousins. The men sat in the parlour on straight-backed chairs all around the room. There was also a writing desk in the corner. The women sat around the large dining room table. There was a summer-kitchen (a small building) just a few yards beyond the back door. Baking, cooking, and canning were done in this kitchen during the warm, summer days. It kept the main house cool and comfortable. During the winter, of course, the kitchen was part of the large dining room, including the wood stove. A convenient pantry was just behind the wall of the stove.

Aunt Elizabeth was busy preparing coffee, buns, cheese, etc. for the afternoon "faspa" or lunch. The dining room table was large, but it took three settings to feed all of us — Grandpa and the uncles first, Grandma and the aunts next, and then it was our turn. Mother had lots of sisters, so there was help to clear the table, wash the dishes, and serve coffee.

We cousins played games. There were lots of places to hide for Hide and Seek. When the Henry Blocks family came, there were enough boys to make up two teams and play ball. It was especially fun when

Uncle Frank and Aunt Tina came to visit. They lived in Saskatoon and owned a store. Uncle Frank always brought goodies. I clearly remember getting a sponge ball coloured red, white, and blue.

During the long winter days, if it wasn't too cold, Father would harness a horse and attach it to the cutter and we'd be off to see the grandparents again. Grandmother always had a bag of white peppermint candies in the writing desk and we'd each get one.

At Christmas time, the uncles and aunts had a special day with the grandparents. Another day it was the cousins' turn to celebrate Christmas at their house. It made us feel special. We were a lot of cousins.

IV. LIFE ON THE FARM

Peter and Justina Bergman's Farm — 1924

The above picture displays the Bergman farm in the Borden district. The house and barn were built during the summer of 1924.

Constructing the buildings was no small feat. Father hired a carpenter and helpers. He also asked Aunt Elizabeth (Mother's younger sister) if she would do the cooking. It took her a while to ponder on this task. Finally she said, "If you let me order the groceries I feel I need, I will do it." Father consented. This was a huge help for Mother. Esther was ten years old at this time.

In the picture below, you can see the kitchen attached to the main two-story section. Father and Mother lived in this kitchen/shanty from the time they got married in 1912 until 1924

Completed House

The kitchen/shanty was very crowded. There was a bed, a crib where Esther slept till she was ten, a stove, a table, chairs, a sewing machine, a china cupboard, a flour bin, a wardrobe, a rocking chair and a chiffonier. As Esther said, "You would wonder if there was any room in the middle to change...your mind."

When the house was constructed, they turned the kitchen/shanty around and attached it to the two-storey section of the house. The one and only door into the house opened into a roomy porch. There was a large dining room, a parlour, and a bedroom on the main floor. Three more bedrooms were upstairs. Now Esther had her own private bedroom with a proper bed. Four years later I came along and three years after that Helen joined us. Following six years later, Alvina was born. She was born in July and that year in November, Father and Mother celebrated their twenty-fifth wedding anniversary.

Life on the farm was always busy. Father hired help to work on the land. Horses were used and later on a tractor with lugs (not rubber tires) did the job. Cows needed to be milked twice a day. It was Helen's and my job to go look for the cows in the pasture and bring them home. We learned how to milk them too. Pigs and chickens had to be fed. We used our wagon to go and get the ground-up feed from the elevator. We could load up four big pails full of feed — two pails on top of the lower two.

This wagon of ours was also convenient to load up with wood to fill the wood-box in the kitchen. The wood stove did an excellent job of baking the bread and buns just right. Mother was a great cook and knew how to bring the temperature of the oven to the right number of degrees for a perfect outcome.

P.P. Bergman Elevator

This elevator was built in the late 1930s. It held all the grain that we harvested. No need for bins. The horses pulled the wagon of grain up the ramp through the large, opened door. A lift tilted the wagon so the grain flowed out through a grate in the floor and into a large pit underneath. The engine was started and it powered the belt with attached scoops to carry the grain from the pit to the top, and then it was directed into the bins for storage.

Work in the house had its routine. Every other Monday the laundry had to be done. Esther took care of the laundry. The washing machine, which had a small motor, was moved from the porch into the roomy kitchen. The exhaust pipe was directed out of the kitchen window. By this time the large copper boiler was on the wood stove heating up the water. A large tub was filled with cold water to take care of the rinsing.

We were fortunate. There was a cistern underneath the kitchen (part of the basement). Father had installed a pump right at the kitchen sink and it was very handy when water was needed. The greasy, dirty overalls needed to be washed twice.

Homemade soap was added to the hot water in the washing machine. The motor was started and the agitating took place. You had to be trained to know how to control the wringer. Bluing was added to the rinse water, which made the white cotton shirts gleaming white. The laundry was hung up outside. With the sun and breeze, it was dry in no time.

After all the water was removed from the machine and tub, it was poured into the kitchen sink where the pipes directed it outside to the north side of the house. All was wiped down and the machine was wheeled back into the porch. The tub was hung up on the wall next to the steps going down to the basement.

Before night-time, the laundry was retrieved from the lines and brought into the house. It was an exhausting day for Esther. Mother was busy with cooking, baking, and looking after Alvina. Helen and I did the dishes, filled the wood box, and took care of errands.

Tuesday was ironing day — Esther's job. Since we did not have electric power, we had a propane iron. It did a lot of hissing, but did a good job. The starched clothes had been sprinkled with water the night before and rolled up. Shirts, dresses, aprons, pillowcases, hankies etc. were made out of cotton (polyester wasn't invented yet) and needed proper ironing. The iron did produce a vapour that usually gave Esther a headache by the end of the day. Mother would be mending.

Viola remembers clearly that we had just gotten a radio. The "soaps" were turned on. Imagine that! *Pepper Young's Family* came on, sponsored by Camay soap. It was the story of an ordinary family talking to each other about their experiences. This was followed by *Ma Perkins*, sponsored by Oxydol laundry soap. Maybe this was where the term "soaps" came from. By listening to these stories, Mother improved her English. She had not had the privilege of getting any schooling in Canada. She was nine when her family arrived in Canada, and being the oldest daughter in the family she was busy looking after the younger sisters and brother. She had nine sisters and three brothers.

Saturdays were extremely busy. Mother would bake buns and bread — four large loaves at a time. Esther would clean — starting upstairs. This included making the beds, dusting, and washing the floors. The guest bedroom was rarely used and the door was kept closed. The hired hand's bedroom had to be cleaned, as well as the hallway and stairs. After lunch, Mother and Dad's bedroom had to be cleaned. The parlour was not used much, but dusting was done and the floor got mopped. Our dining room was large and the floor was washed on hands and knees. By this time most of the baking was done and the kitchen floor was washed too. I washed the porch and front steps.

Then it was time for Helen and me to go and get the cows. I helped with the milking. Then the milk was put through a manual separator, which separated the cream from the milk. The three-gallon cream can was stored in the icehouse behind our house. It was kept cool till Tuesdays and Fridays (if I remember right) when the cream can was taken to the corner — one quarter of a mile west, where the truck came by and took it to Borden. There it was put on the train and taken to the creamery in Saskatoon. Cheques were received by mail. This gave us very convenient cash to be used for groceries and other needed household items.

Mr. Hoffman would bring our mail twice a week and leave it in the mailbox — on the same corner where our cream can was left. If we had letters to be mailed, he would take them to the post office in Borden. The post office was attached to the Smith & McQuarrie grocery store in the town of Borden.

Here's a picture of the store in its current state (2014 — now owned by Steve Foster, whose father, Ted, bought it from Mr. Norman Smith, if I remember right).

Foster's Store, Borden, Saskatchewan — 2014

Every family really appreciated getting the *Winnipeg Free Press* and *Western Producer* in the mail — the two most popular newspapers at the time. The *Country Guide* magazine was also an interesting read. The Eaton's and Simpson's catalogues provided us women with the latest fashions in clothes, shoes, sewing material, household goods, Christmas gifts, and much more. When new clothes were needed, Mother would choose the items and Father was recruited to fill in the order form and write the cheque.

Other times, the family would get into the car and head for the city of Saskatoon, which was a couple of hours away. We would head to 20th Street and find the Adilman's Clothing store. Orders were large and Father would convince Mr. Adilman to throw in a belt or socks free of charge. It was done.

We would go to the Commodore Café for a lunch and after more errands were completed we headed for home. Father would often find a box of bananas that were beginning to over-ripen and bring them home. We rarely had oranges at our house, but apples were always there during the winter season.

V. ESTHER AND ABE REMPEL
WEDDING — OCTOBER 5, 1941

Abe Rempel and Esther Bergman married

The fall of 1941 was an exciting time. Esther had a "beau." Abe Rempel was familiar to us. He was a farmer. His home (inherited from his folks) was near the church. Once in a while, he would preach a sermon. We young folk, enjoyed his sermons and they were never long.

As the younger sisters, we had no clue that Abe was interested in Esther. One Sunday, he walked by our car at church as we were getting ready to go home and told Esther, "I'd like to come over today." What a flurry! Dinner was prepared and the table set for our guest. Abe arrived on horseback. He loved horses and he had a favourite one for riding. That day, he was very nervous. After the meal, Esther was excused and she and Abe went into our parlour for a visit. No one was allowed into that room. At some point, Mother and Dad were asked to join them. I'm sure Abe asked whether he could marry Esther and Mother and Dad said yes.

During the following weeks Abe came on horseback and joined us for supper several times a week. Esther prepared the most delicious pies and desserts.

World War II was still going on and different items were rationed. Sugar was hard to come by. Mother saved coupons for weeks, because a lot of cookies had to be baked for the wedding reception that would take place at the church. Susie Rempel, a cousin of ours, was asked if she would come and stay at our house for several weeks and make all the cookies. She agreed.

A wedding shower took place at our house. Alvina was four years old. When a gift with her name on it was opened and her name mentioned, she thought the gift was for her.

October 5th was the day. It was a Sunday and the regular morning service took place. In the afternoon, the sanctuary was full and a lovely ceremony began. After the service, the young men were recruited to remove the pews (long benches) outside, and long tables were set up. Just a few yards east of the church building, there was a separate building, which was the kitchen. A huge cauldron was built into one wall. It was filled with water, heated up and ready to make coffee for the several hundred folks who would be celebrating with the Bergman family.

Oh yes, the day before — Saturday, it had been arranged that Mother's sisters and sisters-in-law each baked a huge batch of buns. So buns, cheese, cookies, and coffee were served at the reception. It was such an exciting day. In the evening, the uncles, aunts, and cousins came to our house for a hot meal of ham and "pluma moos," which was a chilled plum/fruit pudding.

Esther moved out and we missed her. They did come over often, though, which we all enjoyed. Father had another man in the family.

VI. MOVE TO HEPBURN
1945

For some time Father had been contemplating semi-retirement. Farming was difficult without boys in the family. I was planning to go to Bethany Bible School in Hepburn.

Father and Mother purchased some property in the town of Hepburn, which was about half a block east from the church. An auction sale took place at the farm. We kept a cow and some chickens. The piano also was moved to Hepburn.

A three-bedroom house was built. The following picture shows the house facing south.

Bergman's Home, Hepburn, Saskatchewan — 1945

This was a lovely, comfortable home. Mr. John A. Isaac, a good friend of Father's, built the cabinets in the kitchen. Mother had never had so much cabinet space. In the house, Father prepared the blonded, varnished doors; six of them. What a detailed job! The outcome was beautiful.

A garage was built as well as a lengthy building to house some 400 chickens. Father enjoyed chickens and looked after them well. During the right season, hatching eggs were sold to the hatchery in Saskatoon. Helen, Alvina, and I were kept busy cleaning, sorting, weighing, and crating them. Father set up a lighting system with a timer that lit up the whole building very early in the morning. The chickens and roosters were in a happy place and produced many eggs. This generated cash for the household. Our cow provided milk, cream for us and extra to sell several quart bottles to neighbours. The girls often did the milking and made the milk deliveries.

Father built a fancy picket fence along the front of our property. A much shorter version of the same style fence surrounded the flowers next to house. Viola and Helen had the job of painting the fence white with red tips and red along the inside of each board. That gave us something to do in the summer.

Father also planted many evergreens along the front and east sides of our property. They needed a lot of watering.

Alvina enjoying the snow

Alvina accepted the Lord as her Saviour when she was a young child and rededicated her life when she was eleven years old. She was baptized and joined the Hepburn Mennonite Brethren Church at the age of thirteen.

Voleda Harder, Merla Dyck, Alvina Bergman

In this photo we see (from the left) Voleda Harder, Merla Dyck, her dog, Fido and Alvina. Both Voleda and Merla lived across the street. These are the friends Alvina walked to school with most every day.

Merla Dyck, Marjorie Wiens, Alvina in the back row — (girls in front?)

Alvina's Class, Hepburn School

Merla Dyck provided this picture of the Grade 8, 9, 10 class. Back row left to right:

Willie Block, Henry Boldt, Esther Sukkau, John Braun, Marjorie Braun, Martha Willems, Edwin Kliewer, Anne Giesbrecht, Ruben Voth, Edmond Lowewen, Mr. Kippenstein. the teacher.

Second row: Ruben Andrews, Art Quiring, Helene Neustadter, Doreen Siemens, Erika Unruh, Irene Unger, Phyllis Siemens, Marjorie Wiens, Leona Nickel, Dale VanNess.

Front row: Alvina Bergman, Merla Dyck, Verna Friesen, Ruth Willems, Ruby Elias, Dennis Straus.

Ruby Elias, Alvina Bergman

Viola Schmidt

Merla Dyck, Alvina Bergman — on the way to school

Alvina ready for church

Merla remained a true friend into their adult years. Merla was kind enough to write up memories of their exciting times together. She writes:

"My memories of the Bergmans and Alvina. These are my recollections and may not be accurate.

The Bergmans moved from Borden to Hepburn in 1945, at the same time we moved from Osler to Hepburn. The Bergmans had four daughters — Esther, Viola, Helen, Alvina. I think there was quite a spread in age of the daughters. Alvina seemed to be closer in age to Esther's children and enjoyed their visits.

The Bergmans had their home about a block east of the Mennonite Brethren Church in Hepburn. They had a small farm in town — which was common in those days.

Mr. Bergman planted trees and built a picket fence at the front of the property. Barbed wire surrounded the pasture. He apparently liked color and painted the outside of the house in fairly bright shades.

The Bergmans were very religious and conservative. They lived a quiet, dignified life. I remember the home as orderly, calm, and clean. Everyone learned to work. I believe Alvina told me that the kitchen floor was washed three times a day. The living room was used for guests and special occasions. On the brown sofa, there was always a cushion done in punch-wool — of a dog in a storm.

Peter, Justina, Grandma Derksen

(Note the cushion with the dog. It was special, because it was made by Peter's step- brother John Rempel, who was sick with cancer at the time.)

The Bergmans were deeply religious people. They were very involved in the church. I thought of Mr. Bergman as one of the "Church Fathers." In their home, prayers were said before meals. Each person at the table stood behind his/her chair for the grace.

Hepburn Mennonite Brethren Church — built in 1910, rebuilt in 1917

Alvina was a cute, slightly chubby girl with a pretty face and long blond braids. She had a delightful personality. She was never in trouble. My mother used to say she felt safe when I was with Alvina. She felt sure Alvina would keep me out of trouble too! Alvina could be described as pleasant, agreeable, faithful. She called on me for school each morning- and always had to wait because I wasn't ready.

Hepburn School

Alvina and I spent much time playing outdoors. In winter we wore ski pants and hooded jackets. We like tobogganing. The school had a lovely big wooden slide for toboggans and sleds.

In spring, Mr. Bergman got baby chicks and allowed us to spend time with them. We also used to climb the ladder to the hayloft on the west end of the barn. Fido, my dog (Fox Terrier mutt), was always with us. I have no idea how he got up or down. He would try and find mice. I have no idea what we did up there. I recall on one occasion, we had a fight and Alvina ran for her life. She had no time to take the ladder- but jumped out of the hayloft — landing in a snowdrift — unhurt!

When Alvina was quite young she had an appendix attack and was hospitalized in Saskatoon. Dr. Biro had promised to keep the Bergmans informed of her condition and treatment. When they got there the following day, she had already had surgery. Apparently this type of thing was par for the course for Dr. Biro. Mr. Bergman was unhappy about this. I'm sure the Bergmans would have wanted to explain things to Alvina and assure her that they would be there when she got back.

We sometimes played with dolls — but more often we had a stupid game of pretending that one of us was the mother and rest of us were the kids and had to do what the "mother" said. Things might have gotten out of hand — except that we took turns being "mother." On one occasion when I was "mother," I tied a rope around Alvina's waist and we walked down the street with the ditch full of water between us. I ordered her to jump across the ditch. She was wearing new shoes and refused — so I pulled her through the water. This story was told at my graduation. My mother was horrified.

Some of our teachers were principal J. B. Neufeld, principal P.J. Harder, teacher Peter Klippenstein. There was an enclosed fire escape in the school. In winter it was coated in ice and provided quite a ride during fire drills. The older boys shovelled piles of snow for us to land in. Alvina hurt her back during one of these drills. I believe her parents took her to a chiropractor. Mr. Bergman gave orders that Alvina was not to participate in fire drills any more.

The Bergmans' Jersey cow had a place of great respect for both of us. She was generally in the pasture during the day and in the cow stall at night. Alvina and I used to make pies for her. We mixed chicken feed mash and water in a little dish. I don't think the cow ever showed the slightest interest. Alvina knew that I was somewhat afraid of the cow and assured me that the cow was very dangerous. We always kept our distance. One day we walked through the gate of the pasture and then toward the street. The cow was content at the south end of the pasture. When we got to the north end of the fence, I exited through the barbed wire fence. I saw the cow headed slowly in our direction and <u>shouted</u>, "Here she comes!" Alvina took a dive through the fence, tearing her red coat.

Alvina Bergman, Verna Friesen

Some friends we had in common were Verna Friesen, Marjorie Wiens, Phyllis Siemens. Alvina and I loved bike riding and would sometimes pedal out to Friesen's farm to see Verna. I'm not sure how far that might have been. If we had a bit of money we would sometimes stop at the Red & White (Mr. Wiens' store) for an orange crush.

Alvina loved playing table games, as did my parents and I. She enjoyed spending evenings at our home. I think she especially enjoyed my mother's jokes and humour. She would get right into it and tell some jokes of her own. Those were good times.

Alvina had a beautiful alto voice. She loved to sing and harmonized with ease. I recall walking down the street and singing together. I think we both sang in the choir at church.

Of course, the church was central to all our activities. It was like the central command station of the community. Nothing was done without the knowledge and approval of the church. Mr. Jake Epp (principal of the Bible school) was also the minister when seventeen of us were baptized in the North Saskatchewan River. I believe that was in 1951 or '52.

As we got older we were given more responsibility. On one occasion the Bergmans went to Saskatoon. Alvina and I were to feed the chickens after school. Alvina was given some money to spend _after_ the chickens were fed. We decided to spend the money first. We spent the money for treats right after school. Then we intended to feed the chickens before supper. We got a bucket of wheat in the "cow area" and then made our way through the chicken rooms intending to feed the chickens in the last room first. Well, the roosters were not happy with us. To ward them off we pelted wheat at them — which didn't improve their dispositions. The result was that we were trapped in the end room with empty buckets. We were both quite upset — especially since we had spent the money. Alvina thought we ought to pray. I was convinced we should break the windows and escape. Luckily the Bergmans arrived home and rescued us. Punishment? I don't recall.

The Bergmans had a big black telephone on the wall. We had a great time listening in on "party lines." I have no idea what was so entertaining. When the one listening couldn't keep from laughing, she'd hand the phone over and double up with laughter. We especially enjoyed listening in on "De ola Hodashu" (the old Mrs. Harder) who lived next door to the Bergmans.

When I left high school and attended Bethany Bible School, Alvina still had a year of high school to complete. Although I lived at home (with my parents), as a student of Bethany, I was not allowed to attend local hockey games. Since we lived just across the alley from the rink, Alvina would run across during each intermission to warm up and keep me informed about the game. Quite a system we worked out!

After high school Alvina and I went our separate ways. She went to Winnipeg where she completed her nurse's training, married, and started a family. We kept in touch twice a year — Christmas and birthdays. We seriously reconnected when Alvina started writing detailed letters about her cancer, the treatment, and the side effects of the treatment. For approximately two years life was very difficult for Alvina. She had her work and friends there. Even after she was unable to work she would bake cookies and take them to her colleagues at the hospital. Alvina wanted to live and care for her husband and two young sons. Sadly, it was not to be.

At this time the Bergmans had moved into the Home for the Aged in Rosthern. I lived in Alberta. Whenever I came to see my parents in Rosthern, I would also visit the Bergmans. They lived in one fairly large, partially divided room. Mr. Bergman was quite deaf. He spent most of his day sitting near the window watching people come and go. He usually had his feet on a hassock because "his feet and legs felt restless." He loved showing me things like the congratulatory letters received for their 75th wedding anniversary. He was always talkative and mentally alert.

Mrs. Bergman was visually impaired. She waited on him to tell her who was coming or going from the building and who might be coming to visit them. She was also mentally alert and took over the conversation when he was too deaf to do so.

I visited Mr. Bergman when he was admitted to the local hospital. I found him confused and distressed. I believe he died soon after that.

Mrs. Bergman was moved to the Dalmeny Home. I understand she became totally blind before her death.

The Bergmans were special friends to me."

TRIPS

Henry Bergman girls: Anita, Ruth, Dorothy
Peter Bergman girls: Viola, Helen, Alvina

Henry Bergman was Father's cousin. Their farm was near Dundurn, Saskatchewan. We would go and visit them every year or two.

Bergman Family visits California

In September of 1950, Father and Mother decided to visit their friends in California. Helen, Alvina, and I were privileged to join them.

We drove through Oregon and stopped to see the Nickels in Orland, California. We were in "olive" country. How interesting to see the large trees in the orchards!

We moved on to Manteka, California. Peter's stepbrother, John Rempel and his wife Annie had settled there. John was a banker and Annie worked in a creamery. They did not have children. John was sick in bed with cancer. He was the one who had wool-hooked that beautiful, satin cushion with the dog looking up into the sky. The wool had been brushed to make it look like fur.

The Rempels had a beautiful home. I was very impressed.

Then we were on the highway again heading towards Los Angeles. Our destination was Shafter, where the George J. Siemens lived. They had invited us and were so glad to see us. They gave us a good time.

Peter and George had known each other when they were young kids in Russia and went to school together.

George Siemens, Peter Bergman

VII. VIOLA AND ALFRED SCHMIDT WEDDING — OCTOBER 20, 1950

Alfred Schmidt and I married

Before marrying, I worked at the Red & White Store in Hepburn selling groceries and some dry goods. On days that I could not leave to go home for lunch, Alvina was kind enough to bring me a hot meal on her way back to school for the afternoon. It was much appreciated.

That same year, I got married to Alfred Schmidt on October 20, 1950 by Jacob H. Epp. The wedding took place in the Hepburn Mennonite Brethren Church. Reception followed in the basement of the church. Buns, cinnamon rolls, cheese, and coffee were served.

Alfred and I moved into a suite in Saskatoon. Alfred had a job at an electro-plating shop where he made many chrome tables and chairs. I found a job at Woolworth's during the Christmas season.

VIII. HELEN AND HENRY BRAUN WEDDING — AUGUST 26, 1952

Helen Bergman, Henry Braun married

Helen had gotten to know Henry at school and church. They went to Bethany Bible School where Helen graduated. Henry took a year of normal school (teacher training). They were in love and were married in the Hepburn M.B. Church.

Henry had a teaching position at the Ebenfeld School, not far from Laird and Rosthern. They moved into a teacherage and got settled in.

Peter and Justina Family — 1952 Back row: Alfred Schmidt,
Viola, Esther, Abe Rempel, Helen, Henry Braun
Front row: Ruben Rempel, Justina, Alvina, Peter, Carol Rempel

Alvina is in the middle of the front row. Carol Rempel, Esther and Abe's daughter, is to the right of Peter.

Carol has the following memories of Alvina:

"I remember going to visit Grandpa and Grandma Bergman in Hepburn. While the adults were visiting in the living room, Aunt

Alvina would bring out the dolls and play with me. Sometimes we would go up into the attic. There was a lot of interesting stuff up there. I also remember going in the chicken barn and the hayloft. Ruben and I used to stay at Grandpa and Grandma's house for a week in the summer. I remember picking strawberries in the garden, also Grandma's beautiful flowers.

Aunt Alvina had a bicycle, which Grandpa later gave to Ruben and me. I remember learning how to ride it. Ruben might still have it somewhere in his machine shed.

I also remember Aunt Alvina coming to our place in the summer time. I remember the picture of Aunt Alvina, Ruben, and me and our two dogs, Tippy and Rover, sitting on the peak of the ice cellar roof."

When Aunt Alvina married Uncle Dick, I was in charge of the guest book at their wedding.

Also, when Elvin and I got married, she sang two solos at our wedding."

Ruben Rempel, Esther and Abe's son in the front row to the left, wrote out his memories of Alvina:

"When Carol and I were about five and seven years old, Aunt Alvina would come to the farm for about a week during the summer holidays. She helped around the house and garden — we would pick raspberries and eat most of them. Also among the trees north of the barn were wild strawberries and we'd pick them and share what we picked — mixed with cream and sugar.

I remember her hair being long with thick braids.

There used to be a picture of Alvina, Carol, and myself and our farm dog. We were sitting on the peak of the old ice cellar."

Aunt Alvina enjoyed Christian music. She would tune in a Christian broadcast, which ran all day long. She was a very special aunt. She was interested in what happened in our day's work.

Uncle Dick and Aunt Alvina enjoyed symphony music. They would drive to Winnipeg and enjoy supper — then attend the Winnipeg Symphony Orchestra."

IX. ALVINA — GROWN UP

So Alvina now had the bedroom to herself. She was fifteen years old. She was in high school and enjoying her friendship with Merla Dyck and other students in her class.

Alvina Bergman

Alvina — graduate from Hepburn High School — 1956

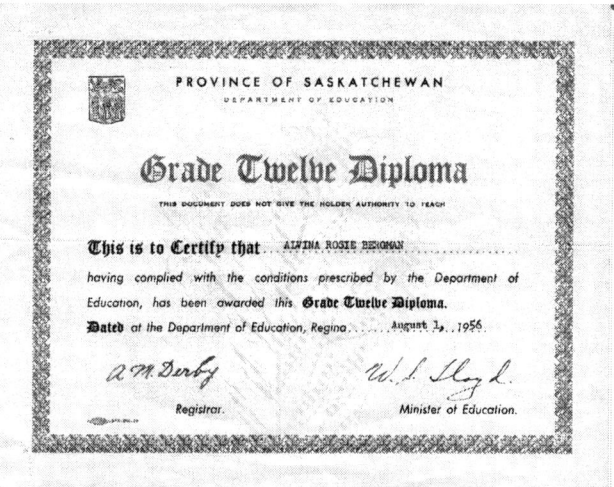

Grade Twelve Diploma

Alvina graduated from high school in 1956 with the ambition of being a nurse. She moved to Saskatoon where she entered nurse's training at St. Paul's Hospital.

Here are the memories of this time from her sister, Helen:

"Alvina had a deep love for the Lord and was willing to take a firm stand for what she believed. This was evident when she could not continue her nurse's training in Saskatoon because of her faith and convictions of what was right."

St. Paul's Hospital was a Catholic Hospital and the priest made it difficult for Alvina, being a Protestant. It even affected her marks.

It was a very sad time when Alvina's dad brought her back home to Hepburn.

Alvina searched the Lord's plans for her. She went to Bethany Bible School in Hepburn for a year. Her yearnings to be a nurse did not go away.

Peter and Justina Bergman Family — 1958 Back row — left to right: Alfred Schmidt, Henry and Helen Braun, Alvina, Abe Rempel, Ruben Rempel, Carol Rempel. Front row, left to right: Me with Rodney Schmidt, Peter Bergman, Lovella Braun, Justina Bergman with Wesley Braun, Esther Rempel, Viola Rempel.

This family picture was taken just before we Schmidts; Alfred, Rodney, and I left for Belgium. We moved into the city of Brussels. Alfred was taking French and history classes about the Belgian Congo. Mennonite Brethren Missions had asked us to teach in the Belgian Congo. These courses had to be taken to qualify as teachers for that country. Karin was born in Brussels. The courses were completed within a year and we flew to the Congo. We settled at the Kafumba Mission station and were teaching in the Bible school. In 1960 the Congo got its independence from Belgium. War broke out and white folks were not welcome. We returned to Hepburn. Alfred was hired as an instructor at Bethany Bible Institute in Hepburn.

Rodney Schmidt, Alvina Bergman, Karin Schmidt

It was a joy to have Alvina come and babysit Rodney and Karin. They loved her.

In 1958 Alvina decided to move to Winnipeg and go to the Mennonite Brethren Bible College.

MENNONITE BRETHREN BIBLE COLLEGE
Winnipeg, Manitoba

Alvina Bergman, (B.R.E.) Hepburn, Sask.

A unique and dramatic personality,
she adds variety in the dorm as well as in class.
She serves the Lord by singing in the hospital.

This inscription is found in the MBBC — 1959 Year Book. Alvina was a freshman in the Bachelor of Religious Education program.

Alvina — Trio — Singing at Hospital

Alvina, to the left, enjoys her practical service by singing in the hospital, spreading joy and praise to the Lord. They also sang at Winnipeg's North End Mission on Main. She continued on for another year at MBBC.

X. GRACE HOSPITAL WINNIPEG, MANITOBA

In 1960 Alvina entered studies at Grace Hospital in Winnipeg in the School of Nursing. She followed her dream and passion.

Grace Hospital — Winnipeg

Adina Pahl was in her class and became a dear friend. Adina's home was on a farm at Sprague in southern Manitoba. Adina invited Alvina to her home on weekends.

A sister-in-law writes:

Alvina and Adina Pahl studied nursing at the same hospital. On a given weekend, they had occasion to be at the home of Gus Pahl, Adina's father near Sprague. Adina's single brother Eugene was still at home. Eugene, not being a shy person, decided it was time to start the day. In a loud voice, he called upstairs, "Skatchewan Shteh Auf!" (Saskatchewan get up!)

Alvina and Adina prepared duets to sing at the service Sunday mornings. Otto Reimer was the pastor at the Sprague Baptist Church and soon convinced Alvina to provide the children's feature — telling them a story. In the audience was the family of Frank Thiessens; Dick, Francis, Andrew, and sisters. Stan Meeks was Dick's good friend. He later married Adina. He told Dick that he would not go wrong to begin courting Alvina. He said, "She cooks, knits, crochets, and stays home." Dick wasn't sure how to go about this new venture. He had not dated girls before. He was kept busy helping his dad farm and cutting down trees in the bush-land. Francis was working together with Dick.

Alvina was about to graduate in the spring of 1962 and she needed an escort. Adina suggested that she should ask Dick. She did ask him and he agreed. Alvina's folks, Peter and Justina Bergman, had driven up from Hepburn, Saskatchewan to witness their daughter's graduation. After the ceremony, they took Alvina and Dick out to the restaurant. Meeting Alvina's parents was a new experience for Dick and he was a bit nervous. Mother Bergman exclaimed, "Oma mensch" (poor soul). To this day, Dick isn't sure what she meant.

Placing of the Cap

THE SALVATION ARMY — WINNIPEG, MANITOBA

Grace Hospital School of Nursing

DIPLOMA

This is to Certify that

Alvina Bergman

has completed the prescribed Course of Instruction and Practice in Nursing extending over a period of three years and has passed the required examinations.

Grace Hospital School of Nursing Diploma — 1962

Registered Nurse — 1967

Part of Alvina's training took place at the Selkirk Mental Health Centre, Selkirk, Manitoba. This qualified her for a position at the Roseau Hospital in Minnesota.

Alvina Bergman — Graduate — Nursing Diploma — 1962

One day Alvina was visiting Dick's family and she was included in a time of devotion and prayer. She heard Dick pray and she knew he was the one for her.

Now Dick got busy looking for a house in the South Junction area. His uncle had a house, but it needed a thorough renovation. There was a wooden foundation so it needed to be redone. There was a well on the yard, so Dick trenched the water into the kitchen. A new roof was put in place.

So the courtship had begun. During the summer Dick had arranged to go up north to work with the construction gang at Grand Rapids working on the hydro plant. He stayed at the hydro compound. Alvina and Dick were writing to each other. Alvina had an upcoming free weekend and she asked if she could come up by bus and visit him. Well, Dick wasn't sure that would work out. The compound was no place for a woman. After much contemplation, he decided to visit the local pastor, Ed Keyler. He was working for the Northern Lights Evangelical Mission out of La Pas. The Keylers were very kind. They invited Alvina to stay with them and to top it off, they offered their car to Dick for the three-day weekend. It was an answer to prayer.

Dick was now twenty-six years old. Alvina was attending the North Kildonan Mennonite Brethren church in Winnipeg. Dick would join her there and take her out to the "Vineyard" restaurant after the service. He wasn't sure what to do for the rest of the afternoon. He suggested going for a boat ride through the Selkirk locks along the Red River. Alvina wasn't sure if her church attire was suitable, so that outing was postponed.

Other times, they would go and listen to the symphony orchestra under the direction of Victor Felderill. The Sunday afternoon's presentation of classical music was very enjoyable.

Now there had been times where Alvina was not sure about her future. She had felt the urge from the Lord to go into mission work. When she asked Dick if he would join her, he knew he did not have the training nor did he sense this calling from the Lord. Thus the courtship lasted some two years.

XI. *ALVINA AND DICK THIESSEN WEDDING — AUGUST 22, 1964*

Dick Thiessen and Alvina Bergman married

The wedding took place in Alvina's hometown of Hepburn, Saskatchewan in the Mennonite Brethren Church.

Alvina and Dick — Wedding Vows

Mr. & Mrs. Dick Thiessen

We witness the wedding and the vows spoken. Alvina and Dick exit the sanctuary with Francis Thiessen, Dick's brother as groomsman and Viola Falk as maid-of-honour following.

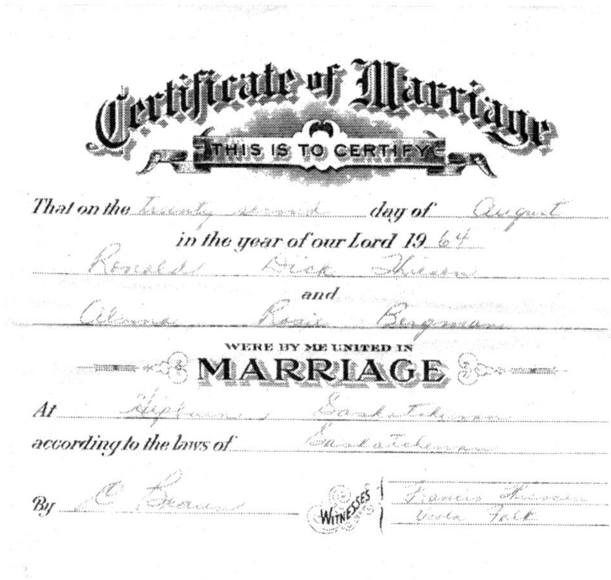

Certificate of Marriage

THIS IS TO CERTIFY

That on the _twenty second_ day of _August_
in the year of our Lord 19 _64_
Ronald Dick Nixon
and
Alvina Rosie Bergman

WERE BY ME UNITED IN

MARRIAGE

At _Neptune, Saskatchewan_
according to the laws of _Saskatchewan_

By _C. Snow_ WITNESSES { _Francis Nixon_ / _Viola Falk_ }

Certificate of Marriage

Wedding Reception, Suburban Restaurant, Saskatoon

The reception took place at the Suburban Restaurant north of Saskatoon. The couple is flanked by Viola Falk and Francis Thiessen.

The couple moved into the renovated house that Dick had prepared. They lived in it for five years.

David, Alvina's son writes:

"In 1964, when Mom and Dad were married, Mom got a nursing job in Roseau, Minnesota, but they lived in a little farmhouse in South Junction right along the Canada/US border. It was on the quarter section just to the east of my Grandma and Grandpa Thiessen's farm (where my dad's brother Andrew lives to this day). The washroom was an outhouse, there was a cellar with a trap door in the floor. Mom apparently insisted on a modern fridge, stove, and washing machine. Drying was still done on the line. My dad told us that the hospital so badly wanted Mom to work there permanently that they worked hard to arrange employment there for Dad too. Apparently this was also discouraged by Grandpa Bergman."

Alvina was always ready to help in the church. She sang solos and she taught the adult Sunday School class.

Francis Thiessen writes:

"Alvina brought a new appreciation for good music and remembering the writers and composers. She was an influence for good in our church and community.

I had opportunity to sample a lot of her cooking. There is one dish that makes me drool today; her chicken tomato borscht made with chicken necks and wings. Yummy.

It was an exciting day in our home at South Junction when we heard that Stan and Adina Meek had introduced Alvina Bergman from some faraway place in Saskatchewan to my brother Dick. Some years later she introduced me to my future wife, Betty Reimer.

What I remember most about Alvina were her fast moving hands and feet. She did not have to say much, her deeds said it all."

Ruben Rempel says:

"I worked for Uncle Dick and his brothers for two winters — probably 1965–1966 and 1966–1967. I stayed with Dick and Alvina in the farm home near South Junction the first winter, then in Steinbach the second winter. Aunt Alvina made it her job to cook breakfast for us. Packed bountiful lunches — often including a thermos of soup and a hearty supper at the end of the day. There was a never-ending supply of sweets and cookies. Needless to say, in spite of working hard, I packed on a few pounds."

South Junction is near the U.S. border. At Roseau, Minnesota, there was a hospital that was in dire need of nurses. Gib Hobbs, who was a customs officer at the border knew about Alvina being a nurse.

He suggested that she should go and apply for work. They checked her resumé, which included some training at the Selkirk Mental Institution and she was accepted for work.

The hospital staff liked her so well they suggested Dick and Alvina should move to Roseau. They began looking at houses. Alvina had written her parents about their plans. Well, after thinking through the whole situation, Dad Bergman said that he was afraid that Dick would be called up into the service to fight in Vietnam and that would leave Alvina on her own. So Dick and Alvina changed their minds and started thinking about moving to Steinbach. Alvina could be working in the Steinbach hospital. Dad and Mom Bergman lent them the money ($5,000) for a down-payment on a house ($15,500) and the move took place."

XII. DAVID BORN — MAY 2, 1966

Before they moved, while still at South Junction, David was born. David writes:

"I think I was 7lb 6oz. That May 2, 1966 was an adventure. Mom and Dad made the trip to Steinbach in a brutal snowstorm in a VW Bug. Dad says he dodged a bunch of deer and they were amazed that they got to Steinbach safe and sound. Roseau MN would have been a much closer and safer hospital to be birthed at, but apparently Grandpa Bergman insisted that this baby not be born in the US for fear of being drafted into the US army in the future."

Dick is a happy dad

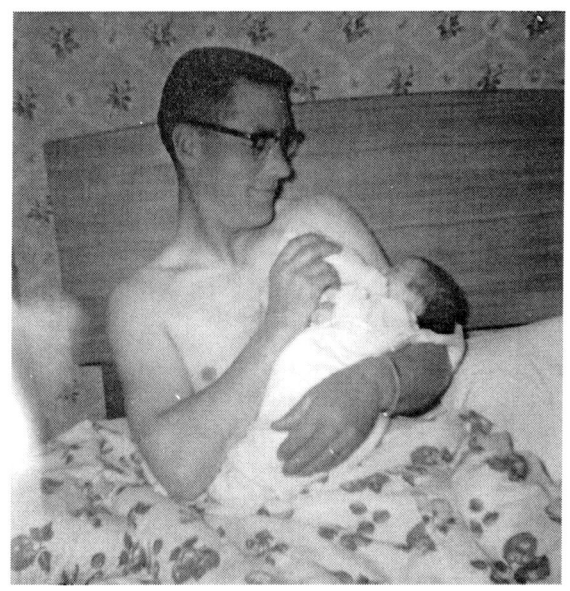

David is content

David — 7 months

David is happy

The move was made. Alvina got a job at the Steinbach Hospital. Most often it was the night shift, so Dick would be home to answer to David's needs.

Dick and his brother Francis spent their time in the forested areas in southern Manitoba. They cut down trees, sawed the logs, and split them to the right size for fireplaces or wood stoves. This provided a livelihood.

David writes:

"Things that very much characterized Mom from as early on as I could remember was for one how extremely well organized she was. She was also the ultimate multi-tasker as I remember and somehow able to work full time and do all the things in the home that mothers and wives do plus many things that many don't do. Mom baked ten loaves of bread per week plus the freezer was never without a supply of cookies and pantry had jam, preserves and the like. I clearly remember her having bread in the oven, running downstairs to throw the laundry in the dryer and pounding out a quick verse of "Onward Christian Soldiers" on the piano before running back up the stairs to attend to something else. If she played a table game with us, it was always while doing something else in the kitchen and she still seemed able to win somehow. She also loved a good game of ping-pong.

I remember Mom having a friend over to play some of her favourite songs on our piano and record them with a tape recorder so that she could sing along to them for special music numbers in the little country church that Mom and Dad attended when they were first married. They would ask her sometimes if she would come and sing. These songs were usually "Over the Sunset Mountains," "Channels Only," and "He Could Have Called 10,000 Angels." These are my favourites to this day."

The Evangical Mennonite Brethren Church in Steinbach became their home church.

Betty Thiessen, Alvina's sister-in-law writes:
"Alvina and I met at our workplace on second floor in the Maternity and Surgical wards. She being an R.N. and I an L.P.N. We had worked together for six years before she spoke to me about Francis, a single brother of Dick.

She was a quick, efficient worker. The patients in maternity loved her for her caring, confident character. Cheerfully, she would hand out bundles of clothing to needy moms.

During our friendship, she and Dick would entertain staff for Sunday dinners, or had staff over for other occasions. I remember her lovely roast beef, mashed potatoes, beets etc.

Betty, Alvina, Dick out for a bicycle ride

Francis and I would ride bikes with them during our courting days. Family times were important to her. She would bring birthday cakes, baked buns etc., for those special occasions.

One evening, after Francis and I were engaged, I suggested to Alvina about practicing the song "If That Isn't Love," which we would be singing together at our wedding. What a surprise, when I walked downstairs where they had the piano, a bunch of staff were sitting there wishing me "Happy Showers." She had a teasy nature too.

She was my bridesmaid, doing a fine job. We used the same pattern for her dress and my gown.

I also admired her skill at working with crafts. How did she ever find time to cross-stitch a picture of beautiful poppies as well as cushion covers, etc.? Or when did she manage to quilt a bedspread that was a masterpiece?"

Alvina's Cross-stitch

Here are the roses that Alvina cross-stitched for me. Instead of a cushion top, Viola had it framed and it is hanging in her apartment living room in Tsawwassen, BC — 2015

Regular trips were made to Hepburn, Saskatchewan to visit parents and family. Peter and Justina had built a new home in Hepburn. Abe, Esther, Carol, Ruben and Viola Rempel lived on the farm that Mom and Dad had built up. Alfred, Rodney, Karin, Randy, Valerie, and I were living in Kajiji, Zaire, Africa. Henry, Helen, Lovella, Wes, Garry, and Cheryl Braun lived in Regina, Saskatchewan.

In 1968 at Christmas time, we Schmidts were home on a study furlough living in Fresno, California. Our parents gifted us with a trip home to Hepburn. We were overjoyed. The children, Rodney, Karin, Randy, and Valerie couldn't wait to see both grandpas and grandmas and uncles, aunts, and cousins.

We all gathered at the new Bergman house in Hepburn for a hearty meal and enjoyable visit.

Dick, Alvina, Helen in background on straight-backed chairs. David in
foreground and Cheryl next to Helen — her youngest daughter

Alvina donned her apron and served. In the back, left to right are
Lovella, Cheryl, and Valerie. Foreground, David, Rodney, Karin

David writes:

"Trips to Saskatchewan seemed to be quite regular, like 3-4 times/
yr. We would oftentimes try to make a loop and see all our relatives
there. I remember overnights at Grandma and Grandpa's in Hepburn,
at the Rosthern nursing home, playing bumper pool with Cheryl at the
Brauns, and I think I remember going bowling once with Val at the
Schmidts'. Overnight visits were also had at Aunt Esther's in the old
house, which was nice since I was quite aware that this was the house
Grandpa built. I remember that house and its layout clearly in my
mind to this day — and the big buffalo head in Uncle Abe's bedroom."

XIII. CONRAD BORN — OCTOBER 29, 1969

Conrad's comments:

"I believe I was born on a Tuesday, shortly after eight in the morning. I was 11 lbs. 7oz. and 24 inches long and breech!

I'm pretty sure that the majority of my size would be due to the fact that I was way overdue. Both my mom and dad had been hassling Dr. Peters (Mom's co-worker and doctor) to induce labour for a few weeks already. My dad must have been in the bush (not sure), but I say that because my understanding was that when Mom finally went into labour, Dr. Peters drove her to the Women's Pavilion in Winnipeg (part of the Health Science Centre) in his own car. So as you can imagine, a breech baby of that size would have been fairly traumatic and it took her quite some time to recover (of course my dad always said that she never did)."

1970

Dick, David, Conrad

David, Conrad, Alvina

David, Conrad

Conrad writes:

"Our trips to Saskatchewan (as I recall), were mostly to Rosthern. We would probably stop in Regina on our way in or out, but not always. I remember that Aunt Helen and Uncle Henry must have lived close to the airport, because the sound of the planes going over at night seemed very scary to me. They had a bumper pool table in the basement (which seemed cool to me) and a little dog (Ginger, maybe?) that would bark and snarl if you waggled your finger, and said 'Granny's chicken.' When in Rosthern, we often took Grandpa and Grandma to church in Borden, which was followed by a trip to the farm. I recall Ruben taking Dave and me to the barn to witness a calf being born. Very interesting!

Before getting to Rosthern, we often pulled over to get the speech: Little boys are to be seen, not heard. When Grandma asks you how old you are and what grade you're in, you look her straight in the eye, and speak slowly and clearly. Then, sit still and be quiet. Not the most exciting time! Night-time prayers were all in German, (which I never understood a word of) and seemed to take forever. However, I was once there by myself in 1981 (I would have been 12) and I had the most interesting conversation with Grandpa. He told me about being neighbours with John Diefenbaker and a few old tales. He also told me about how he had never believed that God would allow man to walk on the moon, but at that time the space shuttle program was in full-swing and with almost weekly launches…he couldn't deny it anymore. Surely it must be true. I also marvelled at how there were little piles of rubbed-off wax in front of and behind where his shoes slid back and forth while he rocked. How long was he sitting there rocking?!? It was also interesting to eat with them in the lunchroom, since there were so many folks there with interesting ailments. One guy had to cover a hole in his neck while he ate cereal, so that the milk didn't run out! Ahh, the things that are noteworthy to a small boy!"

John Diefenbaker, Grandpa and Grandma Bergman at the Senior's Home in Rosthern

Prime Minister John Diefenbaker came to visit Grandpa and Grandma Bergman while they were in the Rosthern Home for the Aged. When they were young, Grandpa and Mr. Diefenbaker went to school together. They would go gopher hunting too.

When the Diefenbakers moved to Borden, the only house (small log home) that was available was on Grandpa and Grandma Derksen's (Justina's parents) land about half a mile east of their farmhouse. They became friends — German was spoken. John's Dad was hired as teacher in the Hoffnungsfeld School in the Great Deer district — some fifteen miles east of the town of Borden.

Years later, that small house was moved to Wascana Park in Regina and was put on display as Diefenbaker's home.

Dick, Alvina, David, Conrad enjoy breakfast at Francis and
Betty's home after Alvina's night shift — 1976

A birthday meal at Francis and Betty's home. Francis in the foreground — his
46th birthday — April 28. Susan Mary, Dick, and Francis' sister in background

A relaxing evening on the swing

Alvina coming or going

Alvina provides a hot lunch for Dick and Francis at Marchand,
Manitoba — 1978 (Flies were a nuisance)

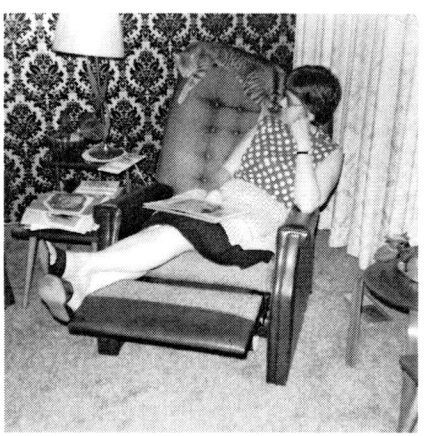

Alvina's favourite chair along with the cat

Alvina, David, Conrad in park

The Sprague Baptist Church invited Dick and Alvina back every once in a while and asked Alvina to sing.

Conrad comments:

"Music was a part of what I remember about my mom! I remember the robe that she wore as part of the church choir.

She had David and I enrolled in piano lessons from a young age and it was her role to make sure that we were practicing and doing our lessons. I can recall countless times when she would be sitting at the piano in the basement playing and singing hymns. I don't think that anyone would have considered her to be an accomplished pianist, but that never stopped her plunking away and lifting her voice up to God in praise.

There were also many times that we would make the hour-long drive to the Sprague Baptist Church, where she would be the guest vocalist. In order to accomplish this she had devised an ingenious method. Mavis Reimer was a pianist/organist at our church who had an organ in her basement. Mom would record Mavis playing the organ with a little cassette recorder and sing the soprano part along with it. Then while playing the cassette back, she would sing the alto part. Essentially singing a duet with herself. I remember 'Gnaden Trone' (Throne of Grace), 'Over the Sunset Mountain,' and 'Ring The Bells' as being her favourites."

More of Conrad's memories:

"Even though she worked full-time (shift work), she still always found the time to keep the house in top shape so that people could stop in at any time and there was no need for a quick tidy-up. There was always fresh baking, cookies, cake, bread, and buns. The cookies in the freezer were always a favourite of mine to sneak while watching some after-school TV.

Television was quite regulated at our house as well. Mom didn't want David and me to be filling our heads with a lot of trash. There were, however, a couple of staples that were usually on the schedule. Lawrence Welk on Saturday and Tommy Hunter on Sunday, together with *Hymn Sing* were regular shows that Mom and Dad watched together.

With being as busy as she always was, there were a few things that she felt were necessary for her to teach me to do on my own. She trained me to get myself up in the morning, make my own lunch, and get myself to school on time. I was regularly taught valuable lessons on how to assist with keeping the house looking respectable (vacuuming, dusting, and of course, raking the shag). All of these were, of course, a very distant second place to making sure that each and every day was spent loving, honouring, and praising Jesus Christ our Lord and Saviour."

David did mention:

"We took several summer vacations as a family. I remember going to Wisconsin Dells, Black Hills, and many weekend getaways to hotels to relax. I think I knew every configuration of hotel swimming pool area of every hotel within a half day's driving distance from home. Mom liked to take pictures with her Kodak Instamatic and these will be treasured for years to come."

AUG   •   73

Alvina, David, Conrad

Alvina, Conrad, David in park

Alvina — summer time

In 1973 my family and I came home from the Congo. We settled in Saskatoon where Alfred attended the University of Saskatchewan working towards a B Ed degree. Rodney and Karin were going to Water Murray High School. Randy and Valerie were at Hugh Cairns Elementary School. Dick, Alvina, David, and Conrad came for a visit and we had the family over. The melamine dishes were used, which had served us well in the Congo. Alvina wanted to give us a gift of china dishes. Eaton's had a good sale on a set for eight people. We were a family of six, so eight would not be sufficient when company came over. Alvina did some research and came up with two sets of eight, which was cheaper than getting extras for twelve or so. These beautiful sets of "Premiere fine china — Rose Garden — 374 Japan" with pink roses/silver trim arrived at our house. Alvina said a silver-trimmed edge matched the silverware better than gold trim. What a wonderful gift! I was overwhelmed. It has been a joy to use them to this day (2015).

On top of that, Alvina bought me a new Felca watch. Another wonderful gift from her, which lasted for many years. Alvina was a "giving" person.

Alvina writes to Esther on March 17, 1975:

"I've been fairly busy recently too. I had people over for meals 7 times in 5 days and I worked all five of those days too. Then I didn't have anyone for almost a week. Sunday — yesterday we had company for supper again. Next weekend we expect people all weekend and more again during school break. I've often wished that my family could just drop in at anytime like that too. I enjoy cooking and company, so don't mind at all if they come.

Otherwise, things are as usual — Dick in the bush, Conrad in kindergarten and David back to piano lessons. I think he will do better now that he is a little older.

Must close for now and make my rounds again. Soon dawn comes — take temperatures, hand out basins, medicines, breakfast etc..."

Karin, Alfred's and my daughter went to Winnipeg Bible College at Otterburne, Manitoba after she graduated from high school. Otterburne was just fifteen miles from Steinbach. Alvina had invited Karin over any time. She would fill her Ford Fiesta with friends and head to Steinbach. Alvina's meals were so-o-o good. It was a great outing.

Dan Block, a cousin of Alvina's, was teaching at Otterburne. He was a favourite teacher among the students. They lived in Steinbach. The church invited Dan to teach a class on "Job." Alvina mentions what a blessing the lessons were. She was planning to have Dan and his wife Ellen over for a meal.

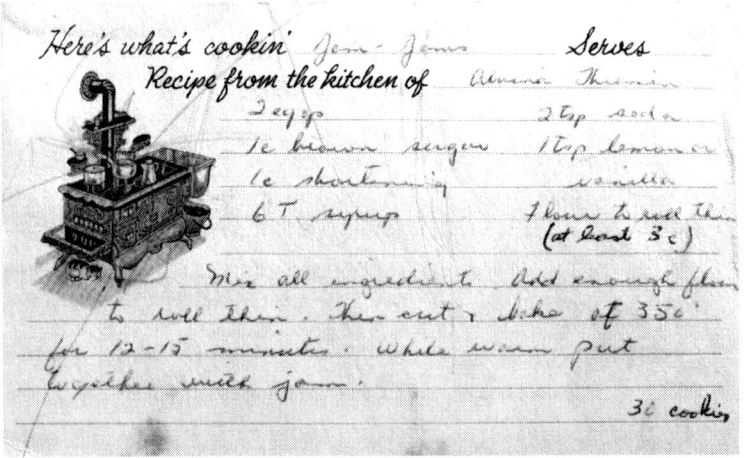

Alvina's Jam Jams recipe

Alvina gave this "Jam Jams" cookie recipe to Viola. It has been used so many times over the years — smudged and scribbled lines by her kids when they were small.

XIV. SAD NEWS — 1977

In 1977 there was sad news. I'll let David explain:

"I do clearly remember the day that we as a family sat around the supper table and Mom and Dad shared the terrible news to Conrad and I. Conrad was 7, I was 11 and what worse news could two boys hear, but that their Mom was sick and the doctors say she could die within 3 months. This, of course became 3 years."

In December, Alvina wrote Esther these words:

"Just a note to let you know that I am doing well. I had my left breast removed Friday as slated. They did a lot of work with the lymph nodes, muscles, and one large nerve. Most of my pain was under my arm and there are still several drains there. Next Friday they plan to remove the right breast in the same process. It is difficult to consent to surgery again, but God does give daily grace and when the time comes the strength will be available again too. I want to go home for a few days between surgeries, but nobody has promised me any such thing.

My room is beautiful. I have 4 beautiful plants and 8 arrangements of cut plants. Also, I have 14 or 15 get-well cards. People do love and care. I have had very much prayer and have really felt much better for it.

My baby-sitter from many years back is looking after the boys this week and my new sister-in-law has helped out with food several times. Yesterday the boys were at her house popping corn while Dick visited me here in the evening."

January 1978 — Alvina says:

"I had my last surgery Jan. 6 and was discharged Jan. 13. Progress this time is very slow. Somehow when I was home between surgeries, I got lots of work done, but now with two painful arms and a very tight sensation across my chest area, I've slowed to a snail's pace. I make 3 simple meals daily and the family does most of the other jobs. We manage amazingly well. They are just so glad I can be at home. My left arm is beginning to show improvement so maybe my right one will soon too.

Yesterday we saw the specialist in Winnipeg. He says I will need much treatment. I begin radiotherapy on Feb. 6 and it continues daily for 2 or 3 weeks followed by chemotherapy. Very soon now, I will be organizing a carpool as Dick does not feel he should be away from his work for 3 weeks. He also said that the next time I was in contact with my sisters to tell them to insist on having their breasts x-rayed as cancer does definitely run in families. A word to the wise. They couldn't seem to impress upon me enough, the seriousness of my condition.

People have been very kind. I received about 50 cards and many flowers. Now we have been blessed with many items of food: brown bread, soups and pies have come in fairly frequently. Above all, people have really prayed. This has helped the most. Please continue to do so.

Today we are having a real blizzard. The temp is -20°Celsius, but at times I can hardly see the neighbour's house.

Thanks for your offer of help, but we do manage. It doesn't matter if I only dust once a week. David even punched bread for me, so we are doing well."

Alvina got twelve volunteers lined up to take her to Winnipeg every day. Dick took her the first Monday and the doctors changed their minds. Chemo was started first for the first two Mondays, then five pills each day for fourteen days. Then she got two weeks off for recovery. The pills cause nausea, but Alvina was not sick — she was lucky. Her arms improved and baking could be done with David's help.

On January 30ᵗʰ Dick's dad was buried. He had been ill often and he was anxious to die. He had a stroke and a heart attack. He was seventy-two years of age.

March 1978, Alvina writes:

"My first week of treatment went very well. The second week, I had a dreadful headache from Monday — Thursday. It felt like my eyes were being crossed in the back. Then Friday the fog lifted and I have been much better again. Last week and this week are my weeks off. I begin again March 7ᵗʰ in p.m. I'll be off all pills Tuesday before Good Friday and if feeling up to it we will probably head for Rosthern. The children are off the following week so we may postpone it for a few days — depending on how I feel the next series. I'm hoping it will not affect me like that again.

Dick is still in the bush. He leaves home at 6 a.m. and returns 6 p.m. They work 50 miles away so spend a lot of time on the road.

My arms have come along real good. I can do all my work — even punching bread. I baked 10 loaves this weekend. I still have not had to buy any. David punched 2 times while I was unable to do it. They enjoy having me home all the time. They would just as soon I never go back to work. Time will tell. I'd rather be well and working.

Otherwise everything goes on as usual. I eat and sleep well. I've gained back all weight lost through surgeries — sorry about that! I've much to be thankful for."

David again writes:

"I remember being 12 years old and being told to take the $50 bill from Dad and the keys to the car and drive by myself uptown to pick up Mom's cancer treatment pills from the drug store. This was 1978. Mom quit the hospital and worked at the old folks home for some reason I can't remember, and it seemed like she somehow worked almost right to the end of her time here on earth.

I remember how sick she was, how she looked after her surgeries, without any hair, and with ugly scars barely hidden by her nightgown that now didn't fit right. One time while I was drying dishes with her washing, she suddenly collapsed in a heap to the floor. She had just fainted from being so ill from all the treatments and stuff. I ran to the neighbour, who was a nurse, for help. She came to and was ok. Many times I had to take the grocery list and get dropped off at the store to do the shopping. I remember one day near Christmas time like most kids I had asked her if I could get some kind of toy for Christmas, and she replied that she didn't know if she'd live that long.

Anyway that's just a bit of the kind of stuff that was hard for a young boy to deal with. Also during that time she was amazing the way she tried to prepare me as the oldest to make sure I knew how to keep the house clean, do the laundry and make all the food that we liked. This all helped, I suppose to make me a more responsible person and prepared to be on my own as well."

As mentioned above, Conrad was also taught how to look after himself and how to get himself off to school.

July 3, 1979, Alvina writes her sister Esther:

"Just a note this time. Thank you for the phone call. It is nice to be remembered.

Like I said, I had a small lump removed from my chest. It was cancer again. Today they also found a much larger one on my throat. I'm starting on pills today and on some form of x-ray therapy — soon — maybe Thursday, but probably Monday. This will mean going to Winnipeg daily for several weeks. I don't know the details yet. Hopefully it will respond to treatments again. I have arranged to be off work all of July and August.

Please continue to pray."

The Bergmans — Last photo — 1979

The whole Bergman family was sad. Her dad and mother in the home in Rosthern. Esther and Abe on the farm, Alfred and I in North Battleford, and Helen and Henry in Regina.

My family and I (except for Rodney and Karin, who would be in university) were packing up to return to the Congo. It was very hard to say goodbye to my sister, Alvina. I was not sure if I would see her again, but Alvina said, "Don't worry, I'll be here."

In October 1979, Alvina wrote:

"Things around here are almost back to normal. The kids are into school and enjoying it. Dick is in the woods as usual. They have an extra man working with them now and he has lots of energy so really keeps them going. He is much younger, slim and nimble with lots of drive. The interesting thing about him is that he speaks no English — only Low German. Dick really struggled the first week explaining equipment and procedures in Low German, but he is clever and only needs to be told once. Bush work in South America is obviously much different than here.

I'm doing fairly well too. I did not go on chemo as planned. The doctors. had just returned from a convention in U.S.A. where they have had very good success with an oral pill. I've been on this pill since July 2nd and am improving. My breathing is getting better. I can even sing along with general singing in church now. In the past few weeks I've had a bad burn to my back where the cobalt is coming through, but this is not as painful anymore so I can lean back into a chair again. I'm working two days a week at the old folks home. This gives me a chance to get out and keeps me active in my profession. Yesterday I had a nice long appointment with the dentist so now my teeth are back in shape again. They really suffered from the cancer treatments, but I'll hang on to them as long as I can. Many teeth are more filling than tooth, but they are my own. That's worth a lot to me.

Today I'm baking bread and doing some cleaning. As I look out the window, I see it is snowing. It has been cold already for several days, which is early for here. I hope it warms up again soon. I'm not ready for winter yet."

Fall: Alvina writes to her sister, Esther and her husband Abe:
"Thank you for your letter. Your place must be like a hive of bees in combine season. Is it all done? I suppose the garden is finished too? We had several hard frosts in the past few days - 20 degrees or so. Dick will dig potatoes today. My vegetables did not do very well, but we did have enough to enjoy — not freeze or preserve. I think the potatoes did well and we need them the most. I sometimes wish we could plant meat, milk and macaroni too. I'm not complaining, only thankful we can afford it and it is still available.

I'm mailing the material to Carol, but thought maybe you could enjoy a cushion top I had lying around. I didn't know what color to back it with so it would go best in your living room. Must close. Love, Alvina"

Dec. 21, 1979 — Alvina writes Alfred and I, who are in Kinshasa, Congo:

"Merry Christmas! Imagine my good fortune I met Mrs. Ben Eidse in Winnipeg on Monday. She knew the David Klassens were going to Kinshasa and suggested maybe I could send along a pound of cheese for you. I phoned this lady and she said I could send a small parcel. It was impossible for me to guess what you might appreciate most. I could have spent 100.00 on groceries and felt good about it, but one small parcel? Mrs. Eidse says prices are out of this world and many things are impossible to buy, but I don't know what in particular and I've never had a chance like this before.

How do you spend Christmas? We have had many programs already with more to come. I've baked enough peppernuts to do us until March. The last 3 weeks I've been busy quilting a bedspread for our queen-size bed. I didn't know it was so much work. It is almost as big as my living room and will occupy that spot over Christmas. We were home (Saskatchewan) in October, so won't be going again. Helen and Henry are flying to BC. Abe and Esther were here in November. We'll phone the folks on Christmas. Dick's side of the family gathers on the 29th, so we'll see a lot of them then.

I am feeling well. My arms are swelling which is new for me, but I feel well. I'm working 3 days a week at Resthaven and will possibly try full-time in February if they can't find more staff by then. Dick is also doing well. The pills seem to keep things under control for him. The boys enjoy school more this year then until now. Conrad has a man teacher, which he much prefers. David thinks grade VIII is much easier then grade VII, but mainly I think it was less adjusting.

When we were home last, Mom and Dad were doing very well. We took them along to visit the Isaac Boldts (Aunt Agnes Stobbe

— Mom's sister) in Saskatoon. Mom was her curious self. Insisted on seeing the whole house, upstairs and down, wedding gown, picture, gifts etc. When I teased her about her curiosity she simply said, 'My eyes are so bad, I want to see everything I possibly can while I still can.' True, her eyesight is failing and can not be improved upon. Must close for now. Do write again. Love and Prayers, As ever — Dick, Alvina, David and Conrad."

Dick, Alvina, David, Conrad (last family picture)

On March 3, 1980, Alvina wrote us that in January she had started coughing and being out of breath. Doing one flight of stairs did her in. Walking one block was almost impossible.

So on January 22 she met with her doctor in Winnipeg and they did an x-ray of her chest. They found much fluid around her heart.

When she took a deep breath they could not feel a pulse. She was put into intensive care and they were able to remove some of the fluid by syringe. Immediately she could breathe better and the coughing lessened.

But major surgery needed to be done to clear all the fluid and remove 60% of the sac around the heart. It was done on Sunday, January 27th. Large drains were put in and during the next week four cups of fluid were drained.

Before she was discharged, they decided to start Alvina on chemotherapy again. It was done by IV and she got very sick. Nausea set in and it was so very painful to vomit having just had chest surgery.

Soon Alvina was back at home and feeling so much better — able to do most of the work around the house. She lost her hair again, but was very thankful to be at home.

Dad and Mother and our sister Esther flew to Winnipeg to pay her a visit. Dad hated flying, but he was quite impressed how easy it was. Esther had taken care of all the details.

Chemotherapy was done intravenously every four weeks. The first evening after that was done, Alvina was retching every twenty minutes and the second day every hour. She felt like she was turning herself inside out. After that, life improved and she was able to do spring cleaning and even some yard work.

But her arms were beginning to swell. She did find out that, "It has spread to my bones — numerous spots on skull, cervical, thoracic and lumbar spine, several ribs and right shoulder blade. Also lumps in the neck area and left shoulder. They are getting smaller so maybe the treatments are helping." (written May 5th)

Dick, Alvina, and boys made a trip to Riding Mountain Park and rented a beautiful cabin. There was an indoor swimming pool and riding stables nearby. The boys had fun and Dick and Alvina relaxed and enjoyed the scenery.

In April, Henry, Helen (our sister) and their daughter Cheryl came to visit. That was enjoyable.

At the end of June Alvina writes:

"Dick was admitted to the hospital with chest pains — not a heart attack, but angina, which they say is due to the hardening of the arteries. He was off work for a while. Now he works shorter days, if he does not feel well, he comes home. The boys go with him at times. David is six feet tall and weighs 215 pounds. He has learned to work the power saw. Conrad drives a huge skidder amazingly well. They are a big help."

Alvina continued with her treatments, but they made her so sick. They were very hard on her heart and her mind seemed to become rather cloudy. It was difficult to remember simple things.

There was much discomfort around and behind the left eye and Alvina was worried about a brain tumour. They did a scan and found none — and she was very thankful for that. The discomfort was due to the deterioration of the bone structure. The chemo was no longer keeping the cancer in check — much less curing it. It was time to try something else.

August 21st Alvina writes:

"Dick and I are going to fly to Toronto August 24th to see Dr. Leo Roy a (so-called) cancer specialist who treats patients with herbs and vitamins. Many have controlled their cancer by this strict diet. I don't know what I have to lose. I believe God can still heal me if it is His will. Maybe He wants me to step out in faith. The church family and my family are behind me in this decision and are praying that my health be restored (if it is God's will)."

Dick had to come home after a week, but Alvina stayed on another week.

During those two weeks Alvina was on a biopulse machine just brought from Germany to help improve the cells' ability to restore themselves. There was only a slight improvement after all that. She came home with supplements of vitamins, minerals, and herbs — taking about eighty pills a day. A six-week supply cost $500.00. She could not eat meat, wheat, dairy products, coffee, tea, sugar, and salt — only fruits and vegetables were allowed.

When she got home, our sisters, Helen and Esther and Mother and Dad arrived to help her. Alvina and Dick met them at the airport. They were so delighted to have them over. Much canning and freezing of garden produce had to be done, as well as baking and laundry. Was that ever appreciated!!

Esther, Justina, Alvina — September 1980 (at Francis/Betty's home)

Dick was taking Vitamin E for his heart condition and he seemed much improved.

After their return to Rosthern, our dad, Peter Bergman, was admitted to the hospital in Saskatoon on October 12th. He had been waiting for this surgery regarding his enlarged prostate gland. He was under observation and receiving tests for a week and the surgery was done

October 20ᵗʰ. Mother stayed in Saskatoon at her sister's, Isaac and Ella Block's home, during this time. She visited Dad every day, which encouraged him a lot. He was doing well.

Alvina and Dick returned to Toronto October 7th. She was having very severe headaches. The coffee enemas did help, but that never lasted too long. The bioscript machine registered that her cells were improving. She returned to Winnipeg with hormone pills in hand to help relieve the pain and her cough, which had gotten worse. She was losing weight.

Dick checked in with Dr. Leo Roy too and found it was his liver that had caused his heart condition. His heart was good.

During all this time the boys were in school and doing well. They must have been coming home with heavy hearts though.

On November 6, 1980, Alvina wrote her last letter of goodbye to me in Kinshasa, Congo in Africa.

"Dear Alf & Vi,

Must take a few minutes and drop you a note. This is indeed a very difficult task. Things are going very poorly in many ways. I'm coughing a lot and often do so until I nearly pass out. I'm also having difficulty swallowing and breathing. It is getting to the point where I am afraid to be alone. There are times when I would like to be admitted to hospital, but I guess the time is not yet. I'm too short of breath to be able to talk on the phone.

The diet consisting mainly of fruit and vegetables was probably a good idea, but for me it was too late. I've been on it right until now, but I can't swallow the pill supplements anymore so will have to give it up.

Dick saw the doctor in Toronto too. He was told to stay off white flour and milk and no pork. This has helped him a lot and he feels very much better.

The children seem to be adjusting very well, they do most of the work. Conrad had a birthday last week and got several cards with

$1.00 in them. Yesterday he took all his money and bought me a bell so I could ring for better service. He is so soft-hearted it often makes me cry. Two nights ago he crawled into bed with me and cried and cried. He is so afraid that I will have to die. It was really hard for both of us.

The church family has really prayed and shown much concern. They helped pay for much of our Toronto expenses too. They often bring in hot soups and pie too.

It seems so many people have prayed for healing but it does not seem like this is God's will. We want God's will and want to trust for daily grace, which He has promised. It is good to know that God understands how we feel when we are even too tired to pray. It is good to know that things were all made clear and settled for the Lord in stronger moments.

The doctor in Winnipeg is talking about admitting me for more chemotherapy and possibly cobalt treatment on Nov. 17, but I'm still not sure I will go along with that. On the other hand when you can't breathe without difficulty, how can you say no? It may just be another one of those hard decisions.

Please continue to pray for us. I'm afraid this letter is rather disjointed — forgive.

We love you very much. If I don't see you again in this life I'll be waiting to see you soon in our home above. John 14.

Love,

Alvina"

Betty, Francis' wife, Alvina's sister-in-law, was staying with her and baking bread and cookies for the boys. Betty says it was very hard for Alvina to be writing all these goodbye notes.

After reading my sister's goodbye, I felt myself drawn to the dining room, where I rested my elbows on the buffet, face cupped in my hands. I looked out the window facing south, searching for God's help. A gorgeous, tropical, black and red bird landed on the bars next to the window not a foot away from my face. It was God's answer for me: "I'm here right beside you and I know what you are feeling. I am the Comforter."

Evie's songs on tape were a favourite of hers. One song really spoke to her at this time:

"JESUS I BELIEVE WHAT YOU SAID YOU'D DO."

Though the world should all forsake me
I will never fear or dread
For you said that You'd go with me
AND JESUS I BELIEVE WHAT YOU SAID.
Though the sky is grey above me
Though I cannot see ahead
Yet You promised that You'd protect me
AND JESUS I BELIEVE WHAT YOU SAID
I believe You really love me
I believe You really care
I believe You died to save me
And as you told me — You'd be there.
When my eyes by tears are blinded
You took my hand and gently lead
Oh, how sweet it is to trust you
For I BELIEVE WHAT YOU SAID.

Alvina was admitted to the Steinbach Hospital Nov. 11th. Gertrude Heinrichs, Dick's closest sister from Rosthern, came and stayed with Dick and the boys for two weeks before the funeral and stayed on another week after that. Helen arrived on Friday and Esther came a day or two later. Alvina was so pleased to see both of them. Helen had to go home on Sunday and Esther stayed on. They all took turns to stay with Alvina. She had to work so hard to breathe. Her lungs were so congested and she didn't have the strength to clear them.

Morphine was provided and she could relax. From Sunday to Monday she had a good night. A special nurse stayed with her. At three a.m. Dick and Esther went to the hospital to be with Alvina. That day she thanked the Lord, "God, You are so good. Thank you, thank you. Thanks for Dick and the boys, for the church and nursing friends."

Several times that day she said, "I love you Dick." At one point she had, with much effort, raised her body to give Dick a hug and whispered, "I love you." After school that day, David and Conrad came to see her. Her face lit up. Conrad said he had gotten 97% in his spelling test. Alvina was so pleased. That was the last time the boys saw her alive. That night just after midnight she gently went to glory. Dick, Gertrude, and Betty witnessed it. Alvina had prayed, "Father, into thy hands I commend my spirit."

Betty asked, "Is Jesus there?" and Alvina nodded her head.

The boys were told in the morning. They went to school, but the principal told David, he and his friend could take some time off. They walked around town and came home. Conrad stayed home because his classmates felt so sorry for him and didn't know how to act normal around him. At night he slept with Dick and cried quite a bit.

After informing Helen and Henry about Alvina's passing, Dick asked Helen if she would let Mother and Dad know.

Alfred and I did not have a telephone, but our neighbours, (the Ellingtons, a quarter of a mile away, had one. That phone number had been passed on to the family in Canada.

Beth Ellington came running to our place with a message saying that Alvina had passed away Tuesday, November 25th. I was so thankful that I had gotten Alvina's letter before all this happened. We also received this telegram a short time later:

"Alvina passed away this morning funeral Saturday November 29, 1:30 p.m. Please call immediately flight arrangements will be made. Telephone 306 596-2650

Henry"

I went to Menno Travel uptown in Kinshasa to arrange for a flight home. The earliest flight I could get would have me arrive in Winnipeg at seven p.m. The funeral was at 1:30. I also needed to get a visa to leave the country and then be able to come back again. That office had already closed for the day. So that could not be done.

My heart and soul were yearning to join the family, but it was not to be. Our daughter Karin made the trip for the family, catching a ride with her Uncle Henry and Aunt Helen Braun.

Alvina had planned much of the funeral, even suggested the type of coffin it should be — not wood, nor grey. A brown suede material was chosen. She wanted to wear her wig, because her own hair had not grown long enough. She chose her dress as well. For the service, Alvina wanted the congregation to sing: "Saviour, Like a Shepherd Lead Us." They played a tape of Alvina singing a solo — "Jesus Led Me All the Way," which she had sung at our mother and dad's 65th anniversary. It was very appropriate at the service. Dick's sister, June sang, "Over the Sunset Mountain," also one of Alvina's favourites.

Pastor Jim Humphries led the service and Rev. Sam Epp gave the message.

This was her obituary:

"Mrs. Alvina Thiessen was born July 2, 1937 to Mr. & Mrs. Peter P. Bergman of Borden, Saskatchewan. She accepted the Lord as her Saviour when she was a young child and rededicated her life when she was 11 years of age. She was baptized and joined the Hepburn Mennonite Brethren Church at the age of 13.

Alvina received most of her schooling at Hepburn, including a year at Bethany Bible Institute. After a year of studies at the Mennonite Brethren Bible College she took her nurse's training, graduating in

1962 as an R.N. She enjoyed her service to mankind through the nursing ministry until the fall of 1977.

In 1962 Alvina was married to Richard Thiessen. Their happy marriage has been blessed with 2 boys, David age 14 and Conrad age 11. Throughout her life Alvina has displayed a positive Christian attitude of praise. Singing in the choir or singing solos was a highlight in her life.

In the fall of 1977 she was diagnosed as having cancer. Her surgeries included bilateral mastectomies and a major chest surgery to remove fluid from around her heart.

Alvina really appreciated her church family's prayer support. She was grateful for all the kindness shown, particularly during the time friends spent with her during her last admission. She greatly appreciated the concern of nursing friends.

She is survived by her husband Richard, sons Dave and Conrad, parents, Mr. & Mrs. Peter P. Bergman of Rosthern, sisters and spouses Esther and Abe Rempel of Borden, Saskatchewan, Viola and Alfred Schmidt of Zaire, and Helen and Henry Braun of Regina.

She went to be with her Lord on November 25, 1980 at the Bethesda Hospital, Steinbach, Manitoba. Funeral service was on November 29 at 2:00 p.m. at the Evangelical Mennonite Brethren Church, Steinbach. Officiating were Rev. Jim Humphries and Rev. Sam Epp."

TESTIMONY OF ALVINA ROSIE THIESSEN

There are no obstacles, which our Saviour's love cannot overcome. To Him mountains of difficulty are as easy as an asphalt road. As Christians we feel we would give anything if only we could in actuality experience life on high places of love and victory here on this earth and during this life. Able always to react to evil, tribulation, sorrow, pain, and every wrong thing in such a way that they would be overcome and transformed into something to the praise and glory of God for ever. As Christians we know that with God there are no mistakes. Even sickness and suffering have been permitted by God as a glorious opportunity for us to react to them in such a way that our Lord and Saviour is able to produce in us little by little His own lovely character. He has made us for Himself and our own hearts can never find rest and perfect satisfaction until they find it in Him. The only way to really learn to know and to love God is to learn to accept day by day the actual conditions and tests permitted by God, by continued repeated laying down of our own wills and accepting of His as it was presented to us in the things which happen to us. By accepting His will, we become more like Him even while we still are on earth. First I must accept His will for me. Isaiah 28: 27-28 says a kernel must be threshed and broken so it is ready for its highest use. As clay in the hands of a potter, so are we to yield to His will (Jer. 18:6). The rarest and finest jewels and gold have been refined by fire. "Dear Lord, help me to accept what you have for me with joy." As long as we are willing to obey Him and follow the path of His choice, we will hear His voice and feel safe. When he hath tried me I shall come forth as gold. Weeping may endure for a night, but joy cometh in the morning. God is able to turn fear into faith (Psalms 23). Nothing is able to separate us from the love of God. Help me to trust completely. God hath not given us a spirit of fear but of power and of love and of a sound mind.

After the service, the burial took place and a lunch was served at the church.

Alvina's Headstone

Pastor Jim Humphries had visited Alvina in the hospital every other day to encourage her and remarked that he had come away being the encouraged one. He is a young pastor who enjoys the young people. He took David out for coffee to comfort him and give support.

When Dick and Alvina went to Toronto, the church put on a fundraising supper to help pay for some of the expenses. They raised $1300.00. Both Alvina and Dick were overwhelmed with the love that was shown.

Dick was so disappointed that Dad and Mother Bergman were not at the funeral. At the time Dad was not feeling strong enough to make the trip and Mother felt she could not go without him.

Here is a letter that Dick wrote to Alfred and me on Christmas Eve, a month after the funeral:

"Today being a very different Christmas Eve, we thought we would do something very different for us anyway, write letters.

Yes, we do have tapes of the funeral. Esther had the presence of mind to ask for four tapes to be made which we did. Esther, Helen and my sister Sadie in the Philippines each have one tape. The one I have I will send along with Elfrieda Schroeder as you suggested. I think it was a beautiful funeral service. I have played the tape to myself several times. It seems I need to hear it for the healing effect it has. No need to send the tape back. I'll be getting Henry & Helen's shortly.

We just returned from a four-day trip to Rosthern and Regina. I felt I had to make that tour this year even though for me at times it was sheer torture. Alvina and I have been along that road so often and there are so many other memories crammed into my head that the highway was often swimming before my eyes. I did my best to hide my feelings from the kids for fear they'd think I was being too emotional and unstable. We got to the folks at Rosthern Sat. evening. They showed us that they still cared for the boys and me. I had been slightly annoyed with them for not having come to the funeral when they could have easily come by jet in less than an hour. I'm sure Karin would gladly have helped them. After having talked with them for a bit, I was able to forgive them. Dad felt his condition was such that he may have died en route or at the funeral. I could see that as a possibility. He does not look well, somewhat thinner since his surgery. I was told, however, he seems improved during the past two weeks.

I had a nice little chat with Henry and Helen, mostly with Helen since Henry was working most of that time we were there. Would say it was the best talk I've ever had with them, helped to relieve some of my pained feelings.

For the foreseeable future we will be batching it here, the three of us orphans. I don't know if Alvina realized it is probably harder on me than the boys. They are being fed, clothed, loved and sent to school, they have security, I have nothing. That may be overstating it, but perhaps you understand my feeling. We've been doing the laundry and cooking. Betty, my sister-in-law did come in once to bake. Right now I feel like a growly old bear, I don't want anybody else in my den or to touch my cubs or my dead female's things!

Several days ago in the evening Conrad was crying for his mother, I handed him a Kleenex. After a while he said, 'Dad, you'd better take one too.'

I love you,

Dick"

Another letter Dick wrote to Karin, January 17, 1981:

"Just felt I must drop you a wee line at this time. It seems I have been cast in the role of letter-writer at our house along with many other bewildering roles.

As long as Alvina was around, I felt so cozy, secure and self-sufficient. Now all that has been so suddenly and irrevocably altered. Letter writing isn't all bad especially when I have such a need to communicate. I wrote to your Bergman grandparents thanking them for their daughter with whom I had had the honour to be with for 16 years. To me she was my wife, sweetheart, mother of my children and good friend. Life goes on. I continue to see Alvina in my children and I love them for it.

The last two weeks I have been back at work, which is probably helping the healing effect. It seems to me the boys are coping very well. I just hope I will be sensitive enough to see their needs.

I was very happy for every one of Alvina's people who came to our funeral and for you too Karin. Thank you for coming. Thank you also for the flowers sent in your family's name.

Even though I will continue to mourn, I still have so many good memories. I just hope I won't live long enough for them to dim in my memory.

With love,
Dick, David and Conrad"

Francis' (Dick's brother) wife, Betty wrote:
"It was a big shock for us when Alvina was diagnosed with cancer. She always wanted to be cheerful it seemed and wanted to encourage others. She came to visit me during this time, when I was a patient at Bethesda. The three years of cancer included surgeries, chemo, check ups etc. She still had people over and she also set up a quilt where neighbours and friends would come to stitch. For a while she even picked up a nursing job at Rest Haven. She was brave and adjusted. When she could no longer work outside the home, she spent time with those close to her heart, Dick, David and Conrad.

After her admission to Bethesda, she lived another 2 weeks, just like the Dr. predicted. Each time I went to see her, she had another Bible verse that was encouraging her. On her final day, David & Conrad came in after school. Thinking back, I can still see her loving eyes looking at them. Sometimes she would say a few words like, 'Am I doing OK?' Later that evening the RN in charge suggested to me that I sing to her. How could I do that? I sang some songs of faith. That, I guess, was my farewell to a dear friend and sister-in-law and sister in the Lord.

Later more family came and near midnight she passed away peacefully. She had been afraid of three things that might happen while dying: pain in the end — did not happen, having intravenous infusion — didn't need to, choking — did not happen. She stayed clear in her mind, like she had hoped to. 'The Lord looks after His own.'"

Betty's husband, Francis wrote:
"Alvina lived her life to the full. I am sure she never once entertained the thought that life on earth would be done so soon for her, but God had other thoughts. Even in dying she was an encouragement to many people. The best to describe her is 'unforgettable.'"

Here are the memories of Alvina that Helen (her sister) wrote up:

"Although it has been many years since my sister Alvina passed away. I have always admired her for several reasons. Alvina had a deep love for the Lord and was willing to take a firm stand for what she believed. This was evident when she could not continue her nurse's training in Saskatoon because of her faith and convictions of what was right. However, she was very determined to become a nurse, so she took her training at the Grace Hospital in Winnipeg.

I believe Alvina was an excellent nurse. Many people remember her commitment to serve above and beyond duty.

At the same time, I believe she was a wonderful wife and mother. Being a nurse she needed to do shift work. She was determined to train her boys to take on responsibilities in the home. Alvina was a great cook and I believe baking was her specialty. I marvelled at how she never skimped when adding chocolate chips to her cookies. She was always hospitable.

She fought cancer so valiantly for a number of years. Then one day I received a short note telling me that she was very tired and that she had severe coughing spells. She was thankful that she had made her decision for the Lord while she was well, because at this point she was not sure that she could have done it.

When Alvina was in the hospital, it was my privilege to sit with her for a while. It was very difficult for her to speak, but she said she was very happy to have me talk to her. It was then that she asked me to read a specific verse from Isaiah. It was Isaiah 26:3 'You will keep him in perfect peace, whose mind is stayed on you, because He trusts in you.' Then she wanted me to read the next verse too. 'Trust in the Lord forever, for in YAHWE, the Lord is everlasting strength.'

Alvina was a picture of perfect peace and obviously it was because she trusted the Lord. She had established her faith throughout the years and she never wavered throughout her illness.

Her funeral was beautiful and God-honouring. Many kind things were spoken of her. No doubt the highlight for me was to hear a tape of her singing, "Beyond the Sunset." I believe this was played at her request. Some day we will join her up in glory where she is already praising the Lord."

Dick told Viola in a telephone call that he had several vivid dreams of Alvina standing in the kitchen looking out the window and admiring the yellow tulips she had planted. They were her favourite. Dick reached over to enfold her in his arms, but she disappeared — it had been so real.

Another time she was in their bedroom standing at the foot of the bed. Again Dick reached out to give her a hug — she disappeared. How disappointing!!

I conclude with David's remarks written in June of 2006:

"To this day I have people tell me "Oh, I knew your mother and she was such a special woman," or "I worked with your mother," or "Your mother was there for us at the birth of our children and we were so thankful for her." It is a blessing to know that people still remember her and that she impacted people's lives in such a positive way.

I hope that this all doesn't sound negative or like pity seeking, because that is certainly not the case. I was, however, very angry with God though as a teen and young adult. Thanking God for all the blessings was hard, to say the least. And yet somehow when Mom prayed she could always say, 'Dear Lord and loving heavenly Father, I come to you this evening hour and praise and thank you for Your greatness.' To me she set an amazing example.

We certainly are products of our experiences and I think that God in His amazing sovereignty knows what we need to experience and learn, as well as how to perfectly use life's events in a way that will benefit us and others. I know that through these things I was more prepared for the times in our marriage when we experienced the loss of

Janie's parents, grandparents and a miscarriage. I have also been able to relate to many people over the years in a way that wouldn't have been possible had I not had the experiences that came my way as a child.

A good friend recently told me that I should pray and ask God for the recall of memories and dreams of Mom and I believe that He has blessed me already in this way."

APPENDIX

XV. ALVINA'S BACKGROUND HISTORY

FATHER — PETER P. BERGMAN

Peter was born January 13, 1889 to Peter and Helena (Harder) Bergmann in Sagradovka, Fuerstenland, southern Russia (now Ukraine). He had an older sister, Helena (we called her Aunt Lena). She remembers living near the water and watching the ships go by.

Here she tells us in her own words:

"Our village was a beautiful place, a very nice big village, with two machinery factories, a store and so on. We lived very close to the waterfront, not too far from the river, where the ships came in. Express ships and we thought they looked so beautiful and seeing the passengers coming out and others getting in. So every day, I don't know how many ships came in. The freighters came in, so it was a very nice place where we lived. I still remember that it was really beautiful."

(*The Hamm Journal* by Abram Bernard Hamm — 2004 — used by permission)

The family was well to do and when Grandfather Bergmann died, Peter and Helena (Harder) Bergmann inherited the homestead, brother Henry Bergmann got the store and sister Mary got money.

Peter's father got typhus fever and passed away which left his mother a widow with two small children, Helena and Peter ages five and four.

After some years their mother married Jacob Rempel, a widower with a family of seven: Jacob, Suzanna, Abe, twins — Peter and Sara, Henry and John. His brothers and sisters got most of their education in Russia. As the boys grew up and farmland was not readily available in Russia, Father Rempel decided to move the family to Canada, where he had heard was lots of open prairie just ready to claim. In 1903 they came across a rough and boisterous ocean and settled fifteen miles north and east of Borden.

S.S. Cymric Ship

(The Hamm Journal by Abram Bernard Hamm — page 154 — used by permission)

Fellows eighteen years and older had the privilege to take home-steads. Peter was only fourteen, so by the time he was old enough, the best land was already taken. Father Rempel claimed the quarter section west of the church. The big lake on it was just right for duck hunting.

Peter went to school three winters — three months each winter. The rest of the time he was needed on the farm. At school, he was the janitor and had to get there early to start the fire in the heater and sweep the floors. He received ten cents a day.

Jacob Rempel Family.

JACOB AND HELENA REMPEL FAMILY

Mrs. Helena Rempel is Lena and Peter Bergman's mother. Lena is behind Father Rempel. Peter to the right of picture. Henry, Peter and Sara (twins) and John are Jacob Rempel's children from a previous marriage. Nick, between the parents is Jacob and Helena's son.

Grandfather and Grandmother Helena (Bergman) Rempel

MOTHER — JUSTINA DERKSEN

In 1905 Justina Derksen and her family arrived and settled in this area as well where the Rempels lived . She was born August 16, 1893 to George and Anna (Pankratz) Derksen in the village of Hochfeldt, near the Don (sp.?) River in southern Russia.

Bremen Ship

When Justina was eleven years old, the Derksen family came to Canada on the "Bremen" ship, arriving in New York and taking the train to the prairies in Canada. Justina had an older brother, Gerhard, and Anna, John, Sara, Elizabeth, Margaret, and Agnes followed her. She did a lot of baby-sitting.

Grandfather had a sister, Mrs. Daniel Thiessen, whose family had already come to Canada earlier. It was nice to have a place to stay while a house and barn were being built for Gerhard and Anna's own homestead.

More people kept moving into the Borden district and church services were held in the homes. Rev. David Klassen was the pastor. In 1908 during evangelistic meetings with Rev. Frank Wiens, a missionary to China, several people accepted Jesus as their Saviour, including Peter Bergman and Justina Derksen. Later a baptism took place in Father Rempel's big lake and they all joined the Mennonite Brethren church.

In time Peter was able to buy some oxen and a few most essential items of machinery to start breaking up the sod. He was optimistic and full of enthusiasm. Having waited until he was of age he did manage to take up a homestead, although it was twelve miles from home and not very good soil. He would hitch his oxen to the wagon, tie the plough behind it, take enough food to last a week and travel out there. He took the wagon-box off its wheels, turned it upside down on the ground and those were his sleeping quarters. Peter told Esther, his daughter, that he never built a little campfire to heat up some food or make a hot drink. He would plough for a while and then let the oxen graze the lush green grass. For the night the oxen were tied to the wagon wheels. Eventually he had ploughed forty acres.

Peter Bergman — 1911

Helena (Bergman) Hamm — 1910, Peter's only sister

Imagine the many lonely hours he spent and how he prayed and dreamt about a girl God would send into his life and how he would establish a home. It was an important decision and the Lord led him to a shy young girl named Justina Derksen. She also had the conviction that this was of the Lord and after consulting with her parents they planned for a wedding.

Justina's wedding dress was navy with blue lace trim and a blue satin belt. Peter's sister Lena sewed it for her.

XVI. PETER AND JUSTINA BERGMAN'S WEDDING — NOVEMBER 24, 1912

It was a pleasant Sunday afternoon on the 24th of November 1912 when these two joined hearts and hands for life. Rev. Klassen officiated. For supper they served "plumi mous" (cold plum soup/pudding), cold ham and all the extras.

Before the wedding, Peter had bought a quarter of land from a man who lived in the United States. This was some two miles from Justina's home. Peter dug several wells before he managed to find good-tasting water. He built a small shanty, which was fifteen feet long and twelve feet wide (inside measurements) and added a little six by six foot porch. Peter's sister Lena sewed up some kitchen curtains and helped prepare the place for Justina. Peter also built a small barn. For the wedding, Justina's parents gave her a fur coat, a sewing machine, and a cow.

By the way, in 1914, the East Borden Rural Telephone Company provided a telephone to most everyone and we were on a party-line. Several of the neighbours were on the same line, but we each had a different "ring." Ours was three short rings.

After we got our radio, which was during World War II, one Sunday in winter it was so cold, no one would dare go to church and put the horses in misery. Peter turned the radio on, rang the general ring on the phone (five long rings) and notified everyone they could listen to the radio sermon. What a good idea! Hardly anyone had a radio in those days.

ESTHER — BORN MARCH 4, 1914

Esther was born on March 4, 1914 in the shanty. (Esther told Viola that when she was small, she was a petite child. Mother was worried what other people would think, so she made Esther wear several petticoats. They were uncomfortable and hot.)

In time Peter was able to buy a few horses. Oh! Justina was quick to remind Esther, "We already had a horse and a buggy when we got married." How nice! They didn't have to go to church, driving an ox. That felt so good. By raising his own young colts his number soon increased.

After a few years, tragedy struck — swamp fever broke out and Peter's horses died one by one. In one year he lost eight. This was depressing and discouraging to say the least. With this disease infection on the premises, it was not advisable to try to get horses again. It seemed that farming had come to a grinding halt. He seriously considered working for Mr. Norman Smith, who owned the general store in the town of Borden. Mr. Smith said, "Peter, I hear money rumbling for you in the distance on the farm." So Peter bought oxen again — lazy guys!

In 1916, Peter's sister Lena got married to Jacob Hamm. They moved to Winkler, Manitoba and farmed there. Lena was now close to her stepsister Sara, Mrs. Benard Enns.

Father and Mother Rempel decided to sell their farm at Borden and also moved to Winkler and settled on a farm.

In 1918 Peter and Lena's mother got sick. Peter, Justina, and Esther took the train to go and visit her. Lena, Peter's sister, was glad to be nearby and checked in on her often and if she couldn't go, her husband took his bicycle and checked in on her.

By the time Father Rempel took his wife to see the doctor in Winnipeg, the breast cancer had spread. One breast was removed and the doctor was not able to remove all the cancer. It had migrated to the liver and Peter's mother was in a lot of pain. She died September 14th, 1918.

Just a note here: This sounds like Alvina's story. Does one inherit these illnesses? No wonder Alvina's sisters were advised to get regular breast examinations.

Peter, Justina, Esther

In 1918 Peter bought himself a tractor to do the field-work. Tractors in those years were impractical for that job. Thanks to a vaccine that came on the market. Dad soon had horses again. They were immunized and just to make sure, they got a booster shot every spring.

However, the tractor was not to be sitting idle, so Grandfather Derksen bought a threshing machine and the two started a threshing business. After some time Peter bought the threshing machine. Uncle Jake Stobbe (Agnes-Justina's sister's husband) and Peter threshed together for many years. Peter liked people and he got along pretty good with a gang of helpers. He was a good talker with a pleasant sense of humour. Justina was kept busy doing a lot of cooking. Usually she had one of her sisters come to help out. It was also in 1918 when Peter surprised Justina when he came home with a brand-new Chevrolet car. It was equipped with curtains. Mother had a slight concern, "How are we going to make all those payments?"

In 1924 after all the debts were paid, they built a new two-storey house. The shanty, which they had called home for twelve years became the kitchen of the new house. Justina was delighted at the amount of space they had now. Occasionally they had company for night in that little home. Esther remembers one time there were eight of them sleeping there. Now a room that size looked small when it was empty, but when you put such things in it: a china cupboard, flour bin, cookstove, wardrobe, crib (Esther slept in it for ten years) double bed, rocking chair, sewing machine, chiffonier, table and chairs, you would wonder if there was any room in the middle to "change your mind." To Esther it was home sweet home. Peter also built a barn that same year of 1924.

It wasn't all "work and no play" for Peter on the farm. The men in the Derksen family went fishing:

Peter — second from right

They played shinny too.

Peter, Justina, Esther

As the house was larger now, strangely enough, so also the family soon increased. Babies were born at home in those days.

VIOLA — BORN NOVEMBER 20, 1928

Esther will never forget the night when Viola was born. All of a sudden she was ushered out of bed, hustled into her clothes, and was going to the neighbours for a visit. They went with horses (cars didn't run in winter) and Peter dropped her off at the end of the lane. He went on to get a neighbour lady who was a nurse and bring her home to Justina. When Esther got to the house there was a vicious dog. She hollered and the dog barked but Uncle John and Aunt Lena didn't notice. Her Uncle John had two wagons loaded with wheat to haul to town in the morning. Fortunately, the front one had two horse-hide blankets on it, so she climbed up and wrapped up in them. The air was crisp and the stars were shining. In the morning she was introduced to a beautiful baby sister.

HELEN — BORN SEPTEMBER 25, 1931

When Helen was born, Viola and Esther were busy digging potatoes and doing the chores.

Peter, Justina, Esther, Viola, Helen Bergman

ALVINA — BORN JULY 2, 1937

Last, but not least was Alvina. She was so new-fashioned that she was born in a Saskatoon hospital — just at a time when Peter was at a general church conference in Manitoba. A telegram came to the moderator and it was announced over the public address system that the Peter Bergmans had a baby daughter. And so it was that Peter and Justina never had a son of their own. Alvina must have liked it there at the hospital because she didn't come home when her mom did. When Alvina grew up she became a nurse.

The year that Alvina was born was the time of the "dirty thirties" when the crops burned up. She was born on a Friday and Esther remembers the Sunday after when they came home from church it was 100 degrees F.

That year Peter and Justina celebrated their twenty-fifth wedding anniversary in November.

Peter and Justina were active in the church. Peter was church secretary for twenty-five years, taught Sunday school for many years and was also superintendent. He was in the committee for the Christian Endeavour programs held Sunday evenings and was treasurer of the Canadian Mennonite Brethren church conference.

All four Bergman girls had the privilege of going to Bible school for two years, and Esther learned only the other week that Peter had been a director of the Bethany Bible School located in the town of Hepburn. Serving the Lord was very important to our parents and so when the girls were anxious to sing in the choir and getting to choir practice meant driving with horses in winter for 3 ¾ miles, it was just too much of a problem. A boy in the family would have made it much simpler. That was one good reason why Peter and Justina retired early and moved to Hepburn. Another reason was that they always needed hired help in summer to run the farm. It was in 1945 that they moved and the girls thought life would be easy going. Peter decided otherwise. He built a poultry house and kept a flock of 400 chickens. Eggs were sold to the hatchery and there were pails and pails of eggs to clean and pack. There was also a new batch of chicks to raise each spring. They also kept a cow and delivered milk. The yard was almost surrounded with evergreens and the young trees needed watering often.

Peter, Justina Bergman — 50th Anniversary — 1962

In 1963 Peter built a second home in Hepburn, which they occupied for nine years. Then he and Justina went to the Home for the Aged for two years in Dalmeny and have resided in the Home for the Aged in Rosthern since then.

Peter, Justina Bergman — 60ᵗʰ Anniversary — 1972

Peter, Justina Bergman — 65th Anniversary — 1977

Peter, Lena, Esther

Peter is sitting with his sister, Lena at Peter and Justina's sixty-fifth anniversary celebration.

Berman Sisters — Alvina, Helen, Esther, Viola

The Bergman sisters performed at their parent's sixty-fifth anniversary program held in the lower auditorium of the Hepburn Mennonite Brethren church in November of 1977.

Alvina sang two solos. Her sons, David and Conrad, recited Psalm 23 in the German language. Karin, Viola's daughter played a piano solo. Esther and Helen were the family historians.

Peter and Justina's wish was to glorify God for His faithfulness.

Peter, Justina Bergman — 70th Anniversary — 1982

Peter and Justina loved getting visitors. To have friends that remembered you and made the effort to come by was a joy.

Peter would read a passage from the Bible out loud so Justina could hear it. She had Age-Related Macular Degeneration and it took away her reading ability.

Peter was still interested in the local news and world events. The radio helped with that.

Peter, Justina Bergman — Seventy-second Anniversary — 1984

Peter and Justina's last photo of their Seventy-second anniversary in November of 1984 at the Rosthern Home for the Aged in Saskatchewan.

Peter passed away at the age of ninety-five years in 1985 in the Rosthern Hospital. Justina then moved in with Esther and Abe in Langham where they were residing. After a couple of years, the Langham Senior's Home had a room available for her. Esther made daily visits. There was a brand-new building for seniors going up in Dalmeny, a neighbouring town. They named it Spruce Manor Care Home. Esther and Abe reserved a room for Justina. She moved in and lived to be 100 years old. Justina passed away in 1993. Both Peter and Justina are buried in the Hepburn, Saskatchewan Mennonite Brethren Church cemetery.

XVII. GERHARD G. DERKSEN STORY

Gerhard G. and Anna Derksen

Justina's Father, (Alvina's maternal grandfather) wrote a story about his own life as it is written up in the *Gerhard G. Derksen Family Book* (printed by Friesen Yearbooks, Altona, Manitoba — 1983)

As we live in Saskatchewan, Canada, where the evenings and nights are very long in wintertime, I have time to reminisce. Often as I lie awake for hours at night, I think of the past. Have I lived my life to the honour and glory of God or to His shame? I have to confess often it's been to His shame.

I want to try and write something of my youth, as the Lord gives me grace and as best as I can remember. "My wish and prayer is that I may do this to honour and glorify my God and that the family may be admonished to walk worthy of the way of the Lord, always resisting the devil no matter how rough the road may become. May the Lord give grace, Amen."

I was born on September 5, 1866. My parents were very poor. They worked for others and saved some money for their beginning. They rented land but the crops failed and they lost everything they had saved. My father had worked for a salesman for nine years and had saved 500 ruble, which was pretty good in those days. My parents were married on December 1859. Even if they were poor, they had never suffered. The mother, Calonic, bought some land in Hersonshen Government for the Molotshna Mennonite people that had no land. They cast lots and my father was among them who got a piece of land. With new courage they looked into the future. In 1873 they moved to their land.

Grandmother from mother's side moved along. She was a cripple and stayed with my youngest uncle.

I was six years old when they moved. Eleven families moved together. The cattle were all in one herd and chased by the younger ones. I begged Mother to let me go with them. Mother didn't want to let me go, but I said I could do it just as well as my brother Henry, who was four years older. Finally she consented and let me go. But, oh dear, I hadn't thought I would tire so soon. We started out before the wagons and so I was always looking back to see if they were coming. I had always been close to Mother and now she was so far away. I was so lonesome for her and started to cry, but no one pitied me and I just had to go on. Finally it was noon and then the wagons caught up to us. You may be sure, there was a little boy who was very happy to see his mother again! He never was tempted again to go ahead with the cattle but stayed close to his mommy. How much it is worth to have a mother who loves and cares for her children.

Such a trip was very hard and tiring for a family. We had to cross a river and wait quite a while because of a storm. Finally they took the cattle on a sailboat and across to the other side. The wagons had to wait till the next day. This trip took ten days. The people with the cattle came the next day.

Father had been there for seeding time, seeding some acres and building a shelter. I don't know about the parents, but we children were very happy to get off the wagons! The whole trip was 200 (verst). It wasn't that far, later we made it in 2 – 3 days.

My uncles, Peter and Henry Pankratz, each had brought a load. Father and these uncles each got a load of lumber for us and then they left for home again. We were left alone with all the work and building. But father was young, strong and healthy and he could work very hard. Right away we hauled stones for the foundation and built a large Mennonite house. The building went very slow as we didn't have the money for it. In fall, the grandparents came to help finish the house so that we could move in for winter. The first year there was a very small crop. The next year they seeded 13 (Desti) and got a very good crop. The price for grain was also very good. The Lord blessed and it was so much easier.

Then the people started thinking about school. My parents gave their front room for a classroom. A neighbour was hired as teacher, who didn't have much education, but they thought he could teach the children to read and write. The next winter we had a different teacher by the name of Paul Peters. He didn't have much education either and we learned very little. The third winter we had a Lutheran teacher who had taught three years already. But they disagreed and fired him. I didn't learn much in these three years as I didn't have any books nor was I taught correctly. I always had to read out of the Katechismus. I don't know if our parents couldn't afford books or if it was just carelessness. Later they built a school and then it was a little better. They hired a Mr. A. Wolk who stayed for two winters. He had more schooling and could explain so we could understand. He moved to America and farmed there. Next they hired a Mr. Henry Plett, who tried his best, but he hadn't written exams so he took evening classes from a Mr. Koehn. This Mr. Koehn also had a private school in his own home for the bigger fellows. There brother Henry and I took classes.

What I hadn't learnt so far this teacher wanted to pound into me. He always hit me on the head with either his hand or a book, two or three times a day. I was all mixed up already and didn't know what to do. We were afraid to tell our parents, but after three months of schooling, my brother Henry couldn't stand it any longer and took courage to tell Mother, who told Father. Then Father went to talk with the teacher. I didn't have to go to his school any more. The rest of the winter I went to the village school and then I was finished with school. I was real happy because for me school was a plague.

Now, about my youth. I don't want to write much of this time for when I think back, I have to bow my head in shame and thank the good Heavenly Father that He didn't snatch me out of this life suddenly. To my shame, I have to say I lived a careless life. The Holy Spirit worked on my heart quite often but I didn't listen. I wanted to live my own life and be happy, not have a long face as I thought I'd have to. My parents often admonished me not to live such a wild life and asked if I didn't want to change. I had to listen to them whether I wanted to or not. They wanted me to get "big." That meant I should belong to a church at 18 years. They asked me to become a Christian and not remain a heathen. I promised but I was sorry to leave the young people and become a long-faced church member. That's what I thought inwardly. But it was like that — whoever announced that he wanted to be baptized and become a member of the church had to live a decent life. Not to hurt my parents I really wanted to live a different life. I knew very well the way I had been living was not enough. The Holy Spirit told me this. One day I mentioned to the neighbour boy that I wanted to be baptized. He didn't think very long till he said he did too, so we decided to go together to the minister, Wilhelm Vothin, No. 5 Nekolaifeldt. My heart was beating fast. We thought he would ask us many questions, which we wouldn't be able to answer. But it was better than we had thought.

He asked if we smoked tobacco. I said "yes." Then he asked if we didn't want to quit. It was hard to promise, but I promised and tried to keep my promise. However, it wasn't easy. I kept away from worldly company. Finally we had to take classes from Easter to Pentecost. We had to learn the Katichismus by heart and recite it on Sundays. We were drilled well. But there was no repentance and confession in us and we were 80 who had requested baptism.

However, I was not careless about this act. The Holy Spirit told me I was not clean and to join the church of God I had to be clean. I had great temptations and no one was there to help me and pray with me. If my parents had been Christians, then everything would have been different. The day came nearer that I should be baptized and I was really scared. The Holy Spirit worked mightily in me and I came to the point where I went to my parents and told them I wasn't ready to make this important step. They were very astonished as they had not expected this. However, they said that if I didn't have joy to do this, I should wait till I had the joy. The next day we went to church and I went right to the pastor's office and told them. They were sorry that I should stay behind but encouraged me that when I was ready they would be willing to baptize me. My heart was so high when I had told them.

However, the burden of my sins was still there. I thought that some day I would be perfect. Instead things just got worse. Soon a year had passed and I hadn't gotten better, only worse. Soon I thought, "Maybe it can't be done — I haven't seen any change in the fellows that had gotten sprinkled last year." So I came to the conclusion to get baptized without repentance. Again I wasn't careless. The sin burden was so heavy, for there were many sins. I often prayed that the Lord shouldn't take me away in my sins for then I would be lost forever. But I stayed the same old person one year after the other.

In Russia all Mennonite boys of 21 years had to serve four years in the forest service instead of going to war. I hated to go for four long years. I was tempted to escape from Russia and go to North America. But my parents discouraged me very much and advised me to be patient and go. If I should be caught escaping it would be much worse. Finally the day came for goodbyes to parents, brothers, sisters, relatives and friends. This was February 27, 1888. It was very hard for me as I had never been away from home before. It seemed very strange to be under strange rulers. But it was better than I had feared. As we got acquainted with the rules and regulations, I tried not to disobey.

Now I want to tell you something about our trip. We were 12 men of our village, Sagradofka, and had to go to the Ratzinische Forest, which was 120 (verst) miles away. By March 1st we were to be there. We went to the village of Schonau and from there we were to be transported by village expenses. We stayed one day in Schonau because of a bad storm. The trip wasn't bad as the roads were good for bobsleigh and horses. But there was a strong wind and one day it blew my cap away. Luckily I had a hood so I could cover my head.

When we arrived, the old soldiers were not there yet since they had all gone home on furlough. However, the house-parents and four fellows were there to greet us and showed us where we should settle down. They gave us a big bag to fill with straw and put on our bedsteads. This was to be our mattress.

The next day 70 more men came. What a greeting that was! I've never seen the likes! Some were quite rough since they had drunk too much. We were timid since we were not used to such a rough life but we had to get used to it. The rulers were very good to us if we behaved well and it was just too bad for those who didn't. They had to learn to obey orders. We had better meals here than we could afford at home. Clothing too was very good and more than we needed. The village had to support us with board and clothing. The government only paid 20 cents a day. Since I had been taught to work at home it was very easy. Some, however, were not used to work and found it very hard. The work was divided evenly among the weak and strong. Since it was a new plantation we only worked 84 days a year. The year ran smoothly.

At harvest time we could go and find work to earn some money for ourselves. This was for two months. In fall the parents signed a petition and asked if their sons could come home for the winter. We were allowed two and a half months at home as there was no work. We were all very happy to go home. What a greeting I got at home and everywhere we went we saw smiling faces and a hearty welcome. We had been away only nine months but it seemed as though they loved us so much more.

Far too soon it was time to say our goodbyes and this time it was even harder. My dear father had been saved while I was away, and now he spoke earnestly to me and the Holy Spirit started to work again in my heart.

The trip back was pretty good. We hired a farmer, Mr. Bernhard Wolf, who promised to take us for three and a half (ruble) dollars each. But he had very poor horses and we wondered if they would take us there. It happened as we feared. After we had gone 50 miles we came to a lot of snow and couldn't go further on the wagon. The other company hired a different team of horses and sleigh, but Mr. Wolf said he had promised to get us there and he would. Then he hired a sleigh and left again.

Our poor animals were soon tired and the others were soon out of sight. The roads were heavy and closed by drifting snow. Our driver walked most of the way and hit the horses. I'm sure he wasn't cold as he often wiped away the sweat from his forehead. We saw that the horses wouldn't make it and asked him to turn back but he was stubborn and wouldn't. Halfway we came to a Russian village where we hired a Russian man for six dollars (ruble) to take us the rest of the way and Mr. Wolf went home. Again we hadn't got the best man — he loved whiskey. Two of our comrades also did and they drank till they lost control of themselves and started to fight by pulling each other's hair. The rest of us had a time to keep them down. Finally he gave us the reins and they slept in and so we had peace.

Twelve miles from our destination we met our fellows, whose horses had also become tired. So the two teams stayed together till we arrived at our place at 8 p.m. We young people didn't take it so seriously, even if things didn't go according to our plans. We paid our driver and in the morning he was gone.

The Spirit started working in my heart again. I couldn't live carelessly anymore. Often I would go and pray. Now my mother had also found peace and joy in her heart and my parents wanted to be baptized by immersion. Before they were just sprinkled and didn't have faith in Christ. In May they visited me for two days, which passed too quickly and the farewell was very difficult. My comrades asked me how I liked it that my parents had gotten baptized again. I said, "They have done the right thing and I know I will have to do the same when I find peace with God."

We were again allowed to go home on furlough for the winter. Soon after we were home something happened in my soul. Since my parents had become Christians there was a completely different atmosphere in our home. Now they had morning and evening devotions. It really worked on me. I always wanted to get saved and had prayed often. But now the Holy Spirit worked so mightily on my heart, I thought it was impossible for me. I thought I had gone too far. I visited the Bible study and prayer meetings and had a great interest in them. One evening as we came home from such a prayer meeting, the Holy Spirit worked so mightily on my heart that I couldn't control myself as they had evening devotions. I broke down and cried to the Lord for forgiveness of my sins. But I didn't accept the forgiveness that soon. I came into very dark hours as I thought there was no hope for my salvation.

This went on for a whole week. Then one day they sang a song, "Suser Heiland, deine Gnade ist viel grosser als man denkt," which means: "Precious Saviour, your grace is much greater than we think." That song struck me so much that I could believe that Jesus had died on the cross of Calvary for my sins. I could personally receive Him into my heart and I was so happy, rejoicing in the Lord! I am still happy in the Lord this day of February 2, 1917 as I write this and I'm not sorry that I took this step, even if it sometimes was dark and dreary. This life is a life of battles but there also are victories.

The Lord then led me to be baptized. I gave my testimony in the village and also in church in Tiegen. My testimony was very weak as I was very nervous. But, the people understood and believed that I was saved. They agreed on a day that I should be baptized — December 25th, 1889. It was very cold: the windows were thickly frosted. They made a hole in the ice and Rev. Richart and I stepped into the water and he baptized me. The people that came with us said a loud "Amen." Some thought I'd catch a bad cold and then they'd get into trouble, because I was in government service. But I didn't, nor did Rev. Richart. I felt like the eunuch in Acts 8:39 — "and he went on his way rejoicing!"

At home I didn't have too great temptations but as I left for government service it was different. For the two years I had worked there I had been one of them — just as wild as the others. Now it was different. I was to be a testimony to them with my life. I must let them know I had said good-bye to the world. Satan tempted me and I would not be able to stand alone. The day before I left for service the people of the village came to say farewell. I told them of my temptations and they all prayed for me and so did I. I asked for great strength to resist the devil and fight the good fight of faith and that I might be victor over the evil one. I found great joy and was very happy with the Christians. Each one gave me a Bible verse or song, which gave me much courage to go on.

The next morning I had to say goodbye to my parents and brothers and sisters. This trip was quite good. We were the first to arrive. Soon everyone came and they were the same as before. They left me alone as if they all knew that I had become a child of the King. I showed them with my life that I had become a Christian; often we four Christians would go in the forest for a time of prayer and reading God's Word and singing songs together. I have learnt many songs off by heart, which was a real blessing in my later years when I was alone in the fields or hauling wheat.

When the year was over we again went home for three months furlough. In the meantime, my parents had moved from Sagradoffka to the Domishen Kosaken. They had sold all the land and the things they couldn't take along. Together with other families they had bought more land. My parents were very concerned that their children should have an easier beginning than they had had.

I went to Sagradoffka to visit my brother Henry and many other families who lived in No. 4. Everyone gave me a hearty welcome! For Christmas I went to my parents. The beginning was very miserable. Some lived in sheep barns. I stayed home for one month then went back to Sagradoffka and back to service for my last year. But before I left Sagradoffka, the Lord led me to my beloved Anna. We promised to be true for life. So it was still harder to say good-bye this time. But it had to be and the Lord gave grace for the trip also.

The life in the forest was as usual but the year seemed very long. If we could have written letters, which the parents would not censor, we could have expressed our feelings to each other. Before the year ended I had an accident, which was especially hard for my dear Anna. As always, my co-worker and I cut wood together and here he cut my right hand half off with his ax. We often had thought of going home as we were in our last month of work. Now I had to go to the hospital for three weeks. Here I had many experiences since it was a low down hospital. They put my hand in a cast, which was very painful. After pleading with them for three days they took it off. After three weeks I could go back to the forest. Everyone was getting ready to leave. Our manager didn't want to let me go as he thought I should wait till my hand was healed. I told him I'd heal it myself and so he let me go home.

As usual, on our trip home the drivers had too much whiskey. They lost their senses and started to race the teams. I begged them to drive decently or they'd have an accident, but they wouldn't. Our driver came into the ditch and tipped over. But oh, then I had pain in my hand; I thought everything had been torn open again. But it wasn't quite that bad and slowly the pain got less. After two days drive we arrived in Sagradoffka No. 1 Alexanderfeld. My hand was still swollen quite badly. My dear Anna had suffered much. I couldn't write her because it was my right hand. She had heard so many stories. Some had told her I could twist all my fingers together; the others had heard my hand was cut off completely. As I took the bandage off and showed her she ran out and cried. She thought it would never heal up right and I'd be a cripple all my life. I had great hopes that it would get better and it has. But it took almost a whole year till I could use it for hard work.

We celebrated our engagement on November 20, 1891. Then we started to visit relatives as was the custom. This we didn't enjoy very much since my dear Anna always had to help me with eating. With one hand I could not manage very well but with love everything is possible.

Our wedding day was on December 10, 1891. It was a very nice day, also very meaningful to us. It took place in my parents-in-law's front room with Rev. Abram Richart officiating. There was lots of singing and playing as many visitors had come.

We celebrated Christmas in Sagradoffka but soon we would have to leave the parents' home. The sixth day of January we left and it was very difficult for my dear Anna to say good-bye to all her family. But it had to be done. There was no reason why we should stay longer. I couldn't help with the work and we wanted to make our home with my parents since Father had bought land for me — 40 Desatinland.

The first day we got to Nikalaidorf where we stayed for the night at Abram Koppen. The next day we went till Kriwaugray, where we took the train to our new home. It was not a pleasant trip for it was very cold -29 degrees F. and the train was heated poorly with only one small heater in the middle. Close to the heater it was too hot and farther away we nearly froze. Finally we arrived at 11 a.m. I hired a Russian man to take us home. He first took us to his place for dinner and I borrowed a fur coat for Anna. We had to drive 40 (verst) miles in -28 degree weather to my parents. Our driver had very good blankets to keep us warm. We had a little trouble as the pole broke while going down a hill but he fixed it quickly and on we went with his good horses. We surprised them when we arrived at 8 p.m. on the twelfth since we had written we would leave on the twelfth. It was a happy greeting! They were all glad that we had made the long trip.

The first year we lived with my parents. Since the house was small, this made it very full. The worst was that I couldn't work. In the fall I could help with the threshing. Anna and I raked everything together. Then we were still threshing with stones. We threshed three loads at a time and three big stones went round and round. My father was away most of the time because of the land. Many of the families were dissatisfied in the village and had lots of quarrels. After years everything cleared up. Instead of paying 47.50 ruble for which we had bought the land, it came to 86 ruble with all the expenses.

The next year my father bought another 44 (Desatin) acres and we could move onto it and live by ourselves. We were very happy! A saying goes like this: "Eigner Herd ist Goldes wert," meaning — being your own boss is worth more than gold! Even if it's only a small mud hut and being poor. We always had enough food and clothing for which we were very thankful. A satisfied heart is always thankful even if it has not much.

Our first son was born on September 16, 1892 when we were still with my parents. We named him George. Justina was born the next year on September 15. It was hard, but we made it.

The Lord has tried us in earthly things. We had four horses and two very good cows, which we had bought quite cheap. I got two horses and a cow from my parents. Two of our best horses died and then a cow. This was hard — we had been so courageous and now this! The crop was small and expenses large. The wheat price was very low. I still remember we bought an old wagon from my parents for 60 ruble. My parents helped us out again with an old horse for 25 ruble. There would be a lot more to write of the eleven years we lived there but I won't.

We then moved to the other end of the village where we bought a very large house, which we had to remodel. The crops were still poor but they started to get better. For six years I had asthma, which was very bad especially in winter. Sometimes I thought I would choke. Often at night I had to go into the barn, hold myself, and gasp for air. I had doctored much but nothing helped. So Anna and I earnestly prayed for healing. I promised God if He would heal me I would give 100 ruble to missions. The Lord was gracious and answered our prayer. I was as well as ever. We praise the Lord for it. We were so poor we thought we wouldn't be able to keep our promise. But the Lord has ways. Our whole village sold out for 112 ruble per acre. We had worked and laboured together for twelve years. We had shared joys, sorrows and hardships. Now we scattered in all four directions.

My parents and us went to Molotshna Colony in the village of Hamburg. We each bought a farm there. For our farm we paid 7,300 Ruble and paid 6% interest on the rest. We moved onto our new farm in October 1903. We brought our seven horses, two wagons and some furniture along. People didn't want to mix since we belonged to the Mennonite Brethren Church and there was none here. So we had to go to Waldheim M.B. Church but we also felt strange there.

We had a very small crop in 1903 and we could hardly pay the interest and the hired man. There was nothing to live on. We saw that in the long run we wouldn't make it and were afraid that we would lose all we had. One lovely morning I came to my dear Anna and said, "Listen, you know what came into my mind? Let's sell the farm."

"And what then? I don't want to go to Tereck," she said.

"Neither do I. My thoughts go to North America." I then went to my parents, who lived across the street and told them our plans. They had nothing against it. I started to believe this had come from God. We received peace and joy to make this move. It was in the beginning of 1905 when I advertised the land.

The buyers didn't show up as soon as we thought. Some came but we couldn't agree on the price. Then a Mr. Aron Warkentin came from Sagradoffka and we agreed on 10,500 ruble. He would take over all the debts, but he couldn't pay everything right away. He wanted to pay 2,000 later. We didn't like this since we felt we surely would need the money to get started in America. So we set a date — if one wanted to back out, he had to send a telegram by then. The day came and I sent him a telegram that the deal was out. But we still wanted to go to America. Then a Mr. Janzen came from Kroknsburg and offered us 10,000 cash money. But I couldn't decide as we had had an offer of 10.500. I offered to split the 500, but he wouldn't give any more so I let him go. Nobody else came.

Spring came nearer and we wanted to go to America. Then one day I said to my dear Anna, "I'll go over to Kroknsburg to Janzens and sell the farm for 10,000." I was lucky to find him home and he was still willing to pay it. But he couldn't give the cash right away so he asked when we wanted to move. I told him in the beginning of May. He said he'd have the money by then. He made a down-payment of 500 ruble and I went home happy.

When I came home I made the auction sale advertisement ready and distributed them on horseback in the villages. In the beginning of March we had a lovely day for our sale. Many people came and the sale was a success. We kept two horses, one cow, one wagon and some furniture, which we sold later. Our whole capital was 8,000 ruble.

Now the time came to say farewell, which was very hard, since we didn't think we'd ever see them again in this world. We never did.

My brother John took us to Alexanderkrohn, to Anna's parents, where we stayed for a couple of days. Here we visited many friends and relatives. It was here that the Holy Spirit reminded me of my promise. I gave the 100 rubel to John Peters who handed it to the mission. From Alexanderkrohn they took us to Priskih where we took the train to Sagradoffka to visit my brother Henry. From here I worked with the papers for the trip and also the pass.

Finally the time came for our departure, which was May 23, 1905. It was a strenuous trip with our eight children; the oldest was twelve years old. We stopped in Germany and stayed four days. In Bremen we took the Hoffmans Hotel and again waited two days. During this time, everything was brought to order and I bought all the tickets for the family for 573 ruble. On the seventeenth of June at 8 AM we took a train to the seaport. It took us one and a half hours. We were then loaded into a small boat, which took us to the large ship. There always was music in the ship. Both sides of the family waved their kerchiefs till we were out of sight.

The tables were set and soon everyone was called for dinner. We always got very good meals — up to eight different things. The name of our ship was "Bremen." On Monday, June 19, we had great winds and our ship began to sway. We started to feel bad but still had good sleep. On Tuesday we fed the fish and Wednesday was really stormy. All the passengers had to go off deck for it was full of water. I asked the employers if they often had such storms. "Oh," he said, "this is no storm! It's just the sea waves." Well I sure wouldn't care to be in a storm! On Thursday the sea was calm again and everyone came out, even the ones who had been seasick. The three eldest children were a little sick.

On Thursday June 27 we looked for land. At 5 PM we landed in New York. Here were so many agencies we hardly knew what to do but the Lord sent us a German-speaking man and we got the trip from New York 94 dollars cheaper than the other agents wanted. After they had checked our suitcases he took us to a hotel where we had to wait a day for our train to go to Canada. On the 28th we left New York. The next day we had to wait eleven hours in Montreal where they checked our eyes again.

We met two German families who were on their way back to Russia. They were not Mennonites but had lived here for four months and found nothing good. They made Canada look pretty bleak. At 9 PM Thursday we left again. Friday and Saturday we went through hills and valleys and two hours before Winnipeg we saw nothing but stones, bush and water. I thought to myself, "If there is nothing better, we might as well turn back!" But Sunday, when we awoke, everything looked different. Everything was so green and fresh. The cattle were grazing in deep grass. This made us feel good again.

We arrived at 10 AM in Regina where we waited another day. We were to stay in the Immigration House but didn't like it so we all sat in front of the door. A German man saw us and asked if we didn't want to come to his house for the night. The Lord again graciously undertook and cared for us. He answers our heart's cry. Here we visited the Salvation Army of which we had heard so much in Russia.

Monday at 10 AM we left again and arrived in Rosthern on July at 9 PM. Here we had to stay in the Immigration House. It was the last night of our trip and also the worst. There were so many bedbugs that we couldn't sleep at all. The children slept but they looked horrible in the morning. I hired a wagon to take us to Wall's, eight miles out of Rosthern. The road went across Carl Glockler's yard and Mr. Glockler asked us where we were going. I told him and he said, "Well, Mr. Wall isn't at home and Mrs. Wall is old. You can stay at our place." So we did. It is wonderful when people are so kind and ask you in a strange land and give you a helping hand. God will reward it. The dear brother helped us so that we could go the rest of the 35 miles over the Saskatchewan River to my sister's, Daniel Thiessen's at Borden. That was a happy reunion after not seeing each other for two years. Mr. Thiessen was just ploughing but as he saw us he hurried home. They had many questions to ask and we to answer.

I have to go back a little. As we were at Glockler's, I bought a horse from him for $150; from his neighbour J. Wiens, two cows at $50 each and two heifers at $25 each. Mr. Peter Voth took us on a wagon to Thiessen's. In Petreifka I bought another horse with colt for $200. Right away we started to farm. The whole trip from Russia to here cost 122 ruble.

The first thing we did at Borden was to visit a sick lady, Mrs. Bernhard Fehr. The next day we went looking for land and soon found some. We wanted to stay close to the other Mennonites. We went back to Rosthern to buy the land and also to get our things. We then bought three oxen and a plough. We started to plough and make hay. First we built a shack (12 by 12 feet) so we could have a place to stay. A well was dug and we found water but it wasn't good enough to drink. So we always had to get drinking water from the D. Thiessens.

Later in the middle of August we started to build the house. Two brothers, Carl and John Ausman, built it for us. They each got $11.50 a day. They dug the well, built the barn (25 by 30), dug the basement and built the house (20 by 30 by 14 feet). All that work for $210.00 — cheap enough! We ploughed 20 acres the first summer and made 35 loads of hay. Winter came before the house was finished. We put a heater up and then it was warm enough to work in. We were so thankful that the Lord gave us health and strength to do all the work.

The church gatherings were in the homes. Often it was in our house. Later the Hoffnungsfeld school was built and we had the services there. After we had bought the most necessary things: furniture, stoves, flour for a year etc., the Russian money was gone. The horse from Glocklers broke through the ice and couldn't get out alone. When we got her out she was still and couldn't get up again. We bought another horse for $100. Then one of our oxen died. It was a hard beginning.

The next spring we seeded 20 acres but got only nine bushels to the acre because it had been broken so late. The spring after that, we broke more land and also some for the neighbour. We ploughed with two oxen and a horse. I also earned some money so we didn't go hungry. Some people from Russia owed us some money and every bit helped. In 1907 we got a very good crop; we should get 1200 bushels of wheat whenever things started to improve. I was chosen as deacon on August 18, 1912.

GRANDMOTHER **ANNA DERKSEN** WROTE IN 1951 (THIS IS ALVINA'S MATERNAL GRANDMOTHER)

I, Anna Derksen, nee Pankratz, was born on September 10, 1871 in Sagradoffka, Alexanderfelt No. 1. My teacher was Heinrich Plett.

When I was fourteen years old we had revival meetings with Rev. Gerhart Siemens. The Holy Spirit convicted me, that I was a lost sinner. By God's grace I found forgiveness of my sins through the blood of Jesus Christ. In 1886 the same year, I also was baptized, together with my parents. They had also been saved. We were received into the Mennonite Brethren Church by Rev. Jacob Richart on July 20, 1886.

On December 10, 1891, Gerhard Derksen and I were married. Rev. J. Richart also officiated at our wedding. We moved to the Domishen Kosaken where we lived for twelve years. Then we sold our farm and moved to the Molotshna Colony in the village of Hamburg. Here we lived only one and a half years and the Lord led us to Canada. In May 1905 we left Russia with our eight children, which the Lord had entrusted to us. We visited our parents and said farewell to all.

In Canada, we soon found a homestead where we made our home. The Lord blessed us! The Lord gave us another five children. They are all saved by God's grace! When times changed in Russia, there came a famine and we could send them lots of parcels of clothing and food to save people from starvation.

The time came when the children got married and made their own homes. There also were sad times. In March 1919, our son-in-law, Peter Rempel (Anna's husband) had an accident. He wanted to go to town and his horses ran away. They ran into the church yard, where there was a large snow bank. The sleigh tipped over and he broke his hip. The neighbours saw it happen and helped him home. It was a hard blow for his wife and us. They doctored him very much, but it didn't get better. For nine years he suffered on crutches. Then the Lord took him Home to Glory in August, 1928. They had four children (two boys and two girls). The youngest was only one year.

Anna was a widow for one and a half years. She then married a widower, Henry Block, who had five children. The children all got saved and live for the Lord. The Lord blessed them with six more children. After eighteen years of happy married life, Anna got sick with double pneumonia on December 13, 1947. She died on the 21st and was buried on December 27. She was almost 53 years old. It was very sad. There was a lot of crying by the family that Christmas. I had been living with them for five years and was sad with them.

Our daughter Sara, Mrs. Paul Wiebe, lived in Herbert. She had a weak heart and lungs. On the 3rd of April she had a stroke on her right side and was speechless. We went to see her on the 4th, but couldn't talk to her and we don't know if she recognized us. It was hard to see her suffer so much. On April 6, 1930 she passed away. She was only 31 years. She left to mourn; her husband and two boys, ages eight and four years. Her funeral was on the 9th of April.

Then, on July 31, 1933, my husband took sick very suddenly. He couldn't pass water. The Paul Wiebes were at our place at that time and I woke him at 5 AM to take my husband to the Radisson doctor. There they took the water but sent him to a Saskatoon hospital right away. The doctors examined him and took x-rays for a week. He had great pain. The Dr. said he had a growth, and they decided to operate. On the 9th of August he had the operation but it was a failure. He lost a lot of blood and got very weak. Then he got the hiccups. They gave him blood, but he continued to get weaker. His stomach and intestines were paralyzed: if he drank a little water, he had to bring it up. Sunday evening they gave him another operation.

Dr. Neufeld then said, "Mr. Derksen, we can't help you." Gerhard asked, "How long will it take?" He was told about five hours. Then he sang the song "Wann schlagy die stunde Ach, wann darf ich gehn Heim nach mein Heim!" (When does the hour for my departure strike to go Home!)

Elizabeth and I were at Frank Peter's place and they called us to his bedside. When we came we heard his loud breathing. He was clear right to the end. He often looked at the watch. I asked him, "Are you going to leave us?" He said, "Yes, let us pray! Oh how wonderful it will be!" Those were hard hours but Heaven was very near. I held his hand till his heart stopped beating and his eyes couldn't see any more. The Lord called him Home! He died August 13, 1933 at 7 AM. The funeral was on the 16ᵗʰ. Many relatives and friends came. He was almost 67 years old. We were married for 42 years. The Lord had blessed us with 13 children. They were all God's children saved by grace when father died.

I farmed for five years after Father's death together with our son Henry. Henry was young but the Lord gave him wisdom and health and we always had a very good working man helping us. The Lord blessed us together with good crops. In 1938 I had an auction sale, sold the cattle and the machinery. I rented the land to the children. I stayed with Henry and Hulda till 1943. (Henry had married Hulda in 1937).

In 1943 they bought land and moved on it and I moved to my children, the Henry Blocks, where I stayed five years. Then on October 11, 1948. I moved to my children, Jacob Stobbe's where I have my home now. Six years ago, the 19ᵗʰ of March, 1943, my son-in-law had an accident. His right hand was cut off in the straw cutter six inches below the elbow. Death was very near. He has suffered very much. He's had three operations on it but with no success. He always has pain in it.

In December 1942, I went together with my children, Henry Derksens, to B.C. They went to their parents and I went to my children, John Stobbe's. I visited many friends and relatives of whom some have gone on to their Heavenly Home. (My husband's sister Elizabeth, Mr. D. Thiessen and Mr. J. J. Stobbe).

The 20ᵗʰ of January 1944, the Lord blessed John Stobbe's with a baby boy named Sam. After nine days she came home from the hospital with pain in her leg. The blood didn't circulate. She got a lot of pain when it went up to the heart. She always had told John that she would die after this baby. They called the doctor. The Lord's plan was different, on February 13 she got a blood clot and she said, "Lord, take me Home!" It was a very hard death. Oh, it was so hard for John and the nine children to be without a mother. The Lord has promised to never leave His children alone. So often we don't understand the ways of the Lord. I've often asked, "Why, Lord?" Margaret was 41 years and 8 days. She was buried on February 20, 1944. From Saskatchewan only the Jacob Stobbe's went to her funeral. In summer I went to B.C. to be a comfort to them.

Our children, George Derksen's also have gone through many hardships, which we cannot understand. I think it was in 1949 when Mary, George's wife, who got this shaking in the nerves which always got worse. In 1944 they went to B.C. but she got worse and couldn't dress herself nor eat by herself. She had lots of pain in her arms and legs. They have doctored her very much but without help.

In November 1947 she got worse and was taken to Chilliwack hospital. She suffered very much and became paralyzed so they took her to the Mental Home in New Westminster. Here she had good care but on January 31, 1949, the Lord called His weary child Home, where she can rest. Often I have prayed and wept and asked the Lord to take her Home. The 5th of February George came to Borden with his dead wife to bury her there since three of his sons live there. The funeral was February 6th. She was 56 years old and they were married 35 years. They had five children; four sons and one daughter.

My father, John Andrew Pankratz was born June 19, 1840. His father Andrew Pankratz died when father was about 14 or 15 years old. He then had to work for his living since his mother was very poor. He found it very hard to be away from home and often complained about the poor meals he got — rye bread and syrup. He worked as a hired hand till he was 25 years old. Then he got married to my mother, Justina Klassen. She was given away for a few weeks to the parents by the name of Dycks, when she was nine years, but she stayed another nine years till she married my father. These Dycks didn't have any of their own children.

My parents lived there for one and a half years and then moved to Furstenlande, Nickolofelt. They had a hard beginning. Here three children died — one daughter as an infant, one of four years, and a three-year-old son drowned. Later they moved to the Molotshna Colony, where they bought a farm in Alexandrathal. Here they lived four years and then moved to Sagradoffka. I was eight years old. Here another died and also a son of nine years. They had another three sons and one daughter born to them. The Lord blessed them so that they had a good living.

My parents got saved in 1886 and were baptized by Rev. Jacob Richart and received into the M.B. Church. Mother died April 30, 19 . She suffered from weak lungs. Father married a Margaret Giesbrecht and the Lord blessed them with a son. I think Father died in 1928. He suffered twenty years from Neroenreizung (arthritis, I think). It was very hard for Mother as Father was often dissatisfied in all his pain. All their property was taken away from them in war-time. He died at 88 years.

Brother Peter and his wife Mary took care of Mother in her old age. Peter was born in 1904 in Alexanderkrohn. Mother died in 1937 and that same year in November Peter was taken away. My sister-in-law has never heard of nor seen him. She was left behind with a little son. Mary's relatives came to see her and took her son Henry with them for a week. But while he was there, they had to escape and they took him with them. We have heard that while they fled, the train in which they were, was bombed and all were killed. Then In June 1928 a baby daughter was born to her. She also had the accident that her arm was broken twice but she didn't lose her arm. In 1948, Mary and her daughter, Betty came to Ontario, where her brothers lived. Here she got work and earned her living.

My brother Henry Pankratz was born March 31, 1877. He married Gertrude Martens and with his family lived in Terrik. When the band came, they had to flee and leave everything behind. They went to Kuban where Henry got work and got started again. They had to go hungry and we haven't heard anything further.

Brother John Pankratz was born May 15, 1881. He had to serve in the C.O. camp. Later he married Maria Bergen of Sagradoffka. The Lord blessed them with a family and property. But sorrow came to them also. His wife died and left behind four children. He remarried and they were very happy. But they also had to flee. I have heard they put him in jail. I am happy to know that John and Peter are saved.

My sister Justina was born December 13, 1883. She was often sick. It was very hard for her when mother died. She was only sixteen years old, but was comforted when father remarried. She married a widower, Mr. Hooge with five children. They were not happily married. After thirteen years she got blood poison in her finger and died.

Brother David was born June 20, 1886. He also had to work in the C.O. camps. After that he married our adopted sister Margaret Giesbrecht. They had two children when she died. He remarried a Sara Heidebrecht. They also were chased off their farm and fled to Kaukasus, where he got work in remodelling a barn. While tearing down a wall, it fell on him and crushed him to death. I haven't heard any more.

CPSIA information can be obtained
at www.ICGtesting.com
Printed in the USA
LVOW07s1440281217
560140LV00002B/1/P